Should I Stay or Should I Go?

*Deciding whether to Stay or
Go and Healing from an
Emotionally Destructive
Relationship with
a Narcissist*

Dr. Theresa J. Covert

Table of Contents

3

Introduction

N arcissism is, by its nature, a tough nut to crack. It's not easy to say why narcissists act the way they do, and there is no singular reason. Within these pages, you will be given a peek inside their extreme inner world, allowing you to better understand their thought processes and motivations.

After spending so much time dealing with the lies of the narcissist, it is time for you to start being honest with yourself. Don't allow yourself to keep up with the lie that the narcissist is going to get better, that things weren't really that bad, or anything else. At the same time, you need to be willing to forgive yourself for the things that happened in the past. If you get yourself in this situation you have to choose between these two options either stay or quit the relationship.

Narcissism is a neurotic condition where the individual encounters incredible challenges inside his relationships, as an immediate aftereffect of hardship endured as a child. The narcissistic practices are the narcissist's self-addictive endeavors to shield himself from any further agonizing narcissistic affront, as experienced as a child, through his unfriendly world, broken school, and family framework. This is his internal directing framework, in a manner of speaking. Since the narcissist does not have the inner structures important to battle their frightening feeling of fracture, tension and declining self-regard, they swing to these outside practices in their endeavor to self-calm. Furthermore, the narcissistic conduct turns into an interminable spiral that continues circling back on itself in each circumstance, bringing about an unending stream of narcissistic casualty misuse.

The following chapters will discuss various tips and tricks that can help you deal with a narcissist in a relationship/marriage.

Narcissists expect people to give them special treatment, so they actively manipulate and control people to ensure that they satisfy that need. Therein lays the problem for most people. If you have narcissists in your life, you can rest assured that they will try to get you to give them special treatment, because they just can't help it.

Knowing more about what might feed a narcissistic personality gives you a greater insight into how to deal with those around you who may have it. Once you can identify the traits, behaviors, and emotions, you have a better handle on essentially what makes the person tick.

It is inevitable that you will run into a narcissist at least once in your life. Just remember that you do not have to just deal with them. There are ways to healthily cope with their behavior so that your self-esteem and life do not take a major negative hit.

This book is going to talk about this very subject and highlight the fact that whilst you might feel like you meet narcissists every single day of your life, a genuine narcissist is actually quite rare. What you're probably encountering is a person who has a generally inflated sense of self-importance, but one trait alone doesn't diagnose someone with a narcissistic tendency!

The thing is, most people have a slight narcissistic tendency at some point in their lives. Sometimes we can be overconfident, sometimes we can put others down needlessly, and sometimes we can seek out validation for no reason. None of this means that we are a narcissist, unless there are several traits together, and it happens on a very regular basis.

You see, a true narcissist is actually a person who needs help, but the problem is that most of them will never admit they need it, and so therefore never really receive it. It's a sad fact, but one which is all too common.

Dealing with a narcissist, especially if you find yourself growing close to one, can be a very difficult situation to be in. You probably won't realize that they are actually narcissistic until you do grow close, because these types of people are masters of disguise. They will appear charming, aloof, and extremely attentive until they have you hooked. From then on, the traits appear, and emotional manipulation takes hold.

A narcissist is someone who suffers from a genuine personality disorder. Despite that, it doesn't make being around one any easier.

This book is going to give you all the information you need on narcissism, and it's also going to help you understand how to deal with one in your life. If you are in a relationship with a narcissist, it may be time to think of yourself and actually get out, if you find that you can't help them, or they don't want to accept help.

It's sad but true that many narcissists are actually very lonely individuals, lacking in self-confidence and not really understanding why people react to them the way they do.

So, whether you have a narcissist in your life, you

think you yourself might have narcissistic tendencies, or you're simply interested in learning more, this book will give you all the information you need.

You do not have to be caught in the narcissist's web of lies and distortions any longer: This book will be your roadmap to mental clarity. You will receive a comprehensive guide on how to cope with a narcissist and how to heal from narcissistic abuse.

If you have picked up this book, it is likely you suspect that you may be actively manipulated by a narcissist at this moment, and you wish to learn more. Please remember, you do not have to accept the abuse of a narcissist, and remember to trust your own instincts and perceptions when around a suspected narcissist. They will do anything in their power to discredit you to yourself in order to continue to manipulate you with zero qualms about it. With the help of this book, you will learn how to disentangle yourself from the narcissist's grasp and begin a journey toward healing yourself from the narcissistic abuse endured.

In these pages, we can find quizzes to assess our own, or someone else's, levels of narcissism. As we go along, we must remind ourselves that, yes, there are healthy forms of narcissism. But for those who have dealt with or have severe forms of narcissism, know this: if you are the victim, you can recover as so many of us have who have gone through what you are going through and come out on top. If you are a narcissist, I thank you for coming along on this journey with us.

At the end of the day, we are **all** human beings and we can **all** change for the betterment of ourselves and for those who love us.

Chapter 1:
Identify and state the problem

Assessing the Situation Objectively

You may be fully aware that you are a source of narcissistic supply, or a target for manipulation or abusive behavior. Perhaps it is clear that you must either break off or continue the relationship. But for those who are still in the questioning phase, unsure about what is happening and the extent to which they need to act, there are several exercises you can do to help you see more clearly.

Abuse checklist

Extreme narcissistic people may be abusive if they are unhealthy enough, as they may be unable to be empathetic to others. If you're unsure as to whether you're involved in an abusive interaction, take a look at the following checklist. Many victims of abuse live in a state of denial regarding the true nature of the situation, making excuses for their loved ones, and excusing their abusive behavior. Abuse can be an insidious process that can leave the victim feeling confused and upset for an extended period after it

13

has finished. It can have crippling effects on the victim's sense of self-worth and confidence and should not be ignored or allowed to continue after it has been identified.

Each type of abuse has various indicators split out in the lists below. If you're unsure about whether you are experiencing abuse, identify which indicators apply to your relationship with the person in question. Multiple indicators mean that it is more likely that what you are experiencing classifies as abuse.

Assessing a Narcissist's Triggers

Assessing a narcissist and what makes them tick can be extremely useful in determining how to best handle them. Depending on your goals, whether these be to survive, thrive, or peacefully coexist, learning their triggers can make the difference between peace and fury.

If you decide not to walk away, it might be an idea to consider purposely becoming less threatening. Avoiding triggering their insecurities, areas of competition, and knowing how to make them feel appreciated can help you to avoid storms and navigate through the waves.

Being true to yourself, is always preferable to

pretending to be something that you are not. However, you may be able to find a compromise, that does not threaten the narcissist, whilst still being true to yourself in important ways. Whatever works for you. For example, self-deprecating humor is consistently applied by the British to make others feel comfortable and to appear non-threatening. Being able to laugh at yourself can put many people at ease. This does not compromise any values of "being true to oneself" as being able to make fun of your flaws is a modest and positive quality.

If you choose to go further, you can avoid talking about (or even downplay) the talents, characteristics and experiences you possess that you think the narcissist will find threatening, and emphasizing your interests and hobbies that they find non-threatening. If you must interact with them, this may be preferable rather than risk invoking their fury and attempts to control or undermine you. It is not a perfect solution, but it is your choice to decide how you need to behave to get what you would like from the situation. Remember that you are attempting to avoid conflict rather than to create it.

Below you will find a guided exercise to assess the narcissist, to help you handle them in the future.

What does the narcissist believe their talents to be?

_____

_____

_____

Is the narcissist competitive in any of these talents?

_____

_____

_____

Have you identified any triggers for insecurity within the narcissist?

_____

_____

_____

What does the narcissist consider to be "non-threatening" in others? I.e. What talents, subjects, etc. do not cross-over into their "realms of importance" in which they need control? Are you heavily involved in any non-threatening areas? These may become safe subjects to have non-threatening conversations about.

_____

_____

_____

Identifying a Narcissist

Narcissists, being master manipulators who love to wear personas to get what they want, can be incredibly difficult to identify at a glance. It takes plenty of interaction to begin to see the behavioral patterns that identify the sneakiest of narcissists. Understanding the narcissist's most common behavioral habits is the first step in being able to identify whether someone in your life is a narcissist. These are behavioral red flags that should catch your attention and prompt you to re-evaluate past interactions with the suspected narcissist. After understanding the most common behaviors, learning the most frequently used manipulation tactics will further your ability to identify narcissists in real life. Lastly, with your understanding of what techniques the narcissist likes to employ, understanding the traits a narcissist seeks in a target will help you understand where you stand in relation to the narcissist. Identifying the narcissist is the first step to mitigating the potential damage that can be done, and ending any narcissistic abuse you may have endured.

The Narcissist's Habits

Narcissists typically have specific behavioral habits they have developed over time that are strongly influenced by the traits that are used to diagnose NPD. They pick up certain quirks and tendencies based on their personality disorder that may first seem like insecurities or abrasiveness, but are actually much more sinister when combined. Some of these can be mistaken for normal behaviors, though a trained eye will be able to notice the difference between sarcasm and malignant sarcasm, or playing the devil's advocate genuinely trying to further a discussion and playing the devil's advocate specifically to inflict emotional harm. By understanding and recognizing these habits, and how they play into NPD, you can begin to take the steps necessary to protect yourself in the future.

The Narcissist's Weapons

As masters of manipulation, it should be no surprise that most have an arsenal of techniques at their disposal. After a lifetime of honing their skills and learning what the most effective is, most narcissists settle on many of the same techniques on their own. This section will detail nine of the most common tactics narcissists use as weapons to get what they desire so you will be prepared to recognize when you are being manipulated. By knowing when you are being manipulated, you are more prepared to take a step back and avoid falling for the narcissist's tricks.

It Wasn't Your Fault

You aren't reading these words because you have done something wrong. You didn't pick this book up because you're stupid or naive. What has happened to you was not your fault.

The aftermath of an abusive relationship is almost as difficult to bear as the relationship itself, albeit in a very different way. After suffering for months or years at the hands of someone who only pretended to have your best interests at heart, someone you loved and wanted to share your life with, something made you realize all was not well.

For many of us, it takes a moment of objectivity, unexpectedly gifted. A moment of clarity in which we can suddenly see what should have been so obvious – and perhaps was horribly obvious to the people around us, who could do little but watch as we suffered. It would have been obvious had it not been hidden under layers of slow acceptance.

In that moment, everything changes. It may have been that your partner went a step too far and broke past your ability to tolerate, it may have been an outside influence showing you what life should be like without this torture, or something else entirely. It's different for all of us.

But whatever causes that moment of clarity, the effect is largely the same. You become aware, hazily at first and then with a sudden jolt, that this relationship is not as normal as you had thought. The way you have been – and are being – treated is not right or fair. This is not the love you thought it was.

For some of us, the backlash is instant and we are out that door in a flash, seeking to place as much distance between ourselves and our abuser as we can. For others, it takes longer to awaken.

Love sets us apart from any other species on this planet. It is the most unpredictable, unknowable and unbreakable force that human beings possess. Smashing through the barrier your own emotions have created isn't easy – and dealing with what's on the other side is just as hard.

Because this wasn't your fault. You did not ask for this to happen to you, nor did you deserve it. Loving another fully and unconditionally is not a sin, nor does it make you blind or idiotic. Whatever blame you have assigned to yourself, whatever painful emotions brought you to these pages, it's time to begin the process of letting go. Your partner does not control your future, not any more. You do.

Are Narcissists Capable of Falling in Love?

Now this is a big part of the equation really. If you want to have a relationship with a narcissist you should know if that narcissist is truly capable of loving you. Well, the first question is if a narcissist is capable of falling in love—that's a good place to start.

And the answer to that question is yes.

Believe it or not, there are narcissists who are capable of falling in love.

Narcissists are human too, so yes they are capable of falling in love. The next question that you need to answer is critical because it is one thing to be capable of falling in love and another thing to be able to reciprocate love.

So, are narcissists capable of reciprocating your love?

The answer to that question is rather complicated. You can say that it is a yes and also a no. There are a lot of factors coming into play and that complicates everything.

For one thing, a narcissist may show affection but on a different level, and also on a different degree.

Remember that their personality can suck out the stability that you have in your system.

Their ego boosting behavior will come into play and there will be times when those behaviors will interfere with the narcissist's ability to fully express his or her love. They are very insecure creatures whether they would like to admit it or not.

Those insecurities of theirs, combined with your emotional entanglements and insecurities, will not always make a lot of well-mixed chemistry. In fact, you should brace yourself for a lot of conflict. Expect a love-hate relationship that is full of turmoil. In fact, narcissists may not even be aware that they are already covering up for their insecurities.

In public, narcissists know how to turn on their charm and attract people. But in the privacy of their home, they are a totally different person. They might know how to say the right words and do the right things, such as telling you caring words, feeding you with compliments, buying expensive gifts, and showing their sincerity.

It is a common misconception that narcissists only know how to love themselves. Their behavior towards other people might make it appear this way, but deep down, they actually hate themselves. Their perfectionism, self-absorbed behavior, and arrogance are often used as a cover for how they loathe themselves. But instead of making themselves suffer because of this, they often project all their anger towards other people. They are emotionally numb inside.

The single biggest thing that keeps women stuck in indecision and how to overcome It - Acceptance

You no doubt have heard the old adage a hundred times before: before you can solve a problem, you need to accept you have one. In the aftermath of an abusive relationship, this applies to you, too.

For most of the time you were involved with your abuser, you felt that the relationship was normal. Everything was fine, for the most part.

Since you can't run away from that narcissist in your life—maybe it's your spouse, your best friend, your parents, or maybe a sibling—your next logical course of action is to accept the fact that you do have to deal with it.

You can limit your interactions. That is all well and good. However, you should also plan for those small moments when you have to interact with them. You should also create contingency plans in case they also interact with your children or your husband or wife.

If it is your spouse that is a narcissist, you should have contingency plans and ways to explain to your kids why you have to separate.

You have to come to terms with the difficult fact that the narcissists won't be able to reciprocate the good things that you have done for them. You will be misunderstood at times and people around you might misunderstand you as well -- and sometimes that is more painful.

Awareness and acceptance is the hard and tough road that everyone in a relationship with a narcissist must tread on. It's a tough one simply because it is hard to believe that your relationship was a lie.

Do some introspection. Ask yourself—is the behavior of your narcissistic husband the same or in any way similar to that of your parents? Do you feel like you are attracted to people who have that strange sense of entitlement?

Are you easily compelled to follow the lead of such a person? Note that it is very easy for sensitive people to feel compelled by narcissists. However, note how it eventually feels inside with that person.

You don't feel good about yourself, right? If you end

up not feeling great about yourself, feeling like you're praising him more than uplifting yourself, then there must be something wrong.

If your spouse is a narcissist and the relationship is choking the life out of you, then get out of that relationship fast.

Remember that narcissists will never think that they are wrong. They will always put the blame on you. They will always think that you are the problem. In the end, you'll just feel like a doormat.

Acceptance is the more difficult path, but it is your first step to freedom.

Acceptance also means that you start believing that you deserve more than what your narcissist is giving to you right now. It is the first step to truly loving yourself.

Whether you justified your ex's bad behavior one day at a time and slowly slipped deeper into the mire, or it was so subtle that you barely even noticed it happening, the larger part of your mind accepted the relationship and all the damage it was doing to you.

Before you can begin to repair that damage, you first need to take the time to understand and accept that this was not a normal relationship. It did not follow the normal rules. Your feelings about how "well" you did in pleasing your partner do not count as normal.

In a normal relationship, you see, there is always give and take. You do your best to make your partner happy and they do the same thing for you. When mistakes are made, they are generally honest mistakes; when behavior is bad, it can be accepted as bad and altered or apologized for. You and your lover are on even footing, respecting, liking and loving one another equally.

That's not the case in an abusive relationship. Part of the game your abuser played was to strip your sense of identity for you and quash your self esteem, with the end goal of making you dependent on them, and only them, and obedient to their view of who and what you should be. All the while they were going about this, you were working under the assumption that you were on the even footing you would be in any other relationship – right up until the end, until your awakening, that's the way you continued to feel.

It's precisely because you thought you were working from an even footing that the damage can be so deep. When your abuser threw accusations at you, told you that problems were all your fault and made you feel worthless, you took it on board exactly as you would had the two of you been on that even footing. One of the effects of being in a narcissistic relationship is that you lose your sense of identity.

So Where Did They Go Wrong?

This is a fair question, because it answers the deep driving need that you have inside of you right now to know whether or not there's any redemption for people like this. Where did they go wrong and is there any way to fix this? Sure, there are lots of ways to fix this and we all know exactly when things went wrong. They went wrong with your childhood and this is the sort of earth shattering thing that we all went through.

Narcissists are told from day one that they are the center of the world and that they can do no wrong and that message is never stopped. In fact, when parents wear out their welcome in the narcissist's life, they seek that validation elsewhere. The only way to know that you're on top of the world and that you're the best is if someone tells you that you are. That's the ugly truth that they come to learn, willingly or no. They will claim that they've 'earned it' which they might have, but not to the degree that they believe. Narcissists all go through this and believe that the world owes them the favors that the rest of the world has already come to learn.

27

Chapter 2:
Present the solution

Your Starting Point

Figuring out how emotional abuse has affected you is not just important on your road to recovery. It will help you spot the hurdles you'll need to overcome as you bring yourself back to emotional health, but it will also do something else: help you avoid a repeat of this torment in the future.

The "symptoms" of emotional abuse begin to appear long before we make that tough decision to escape the situation. They are born during the abuse itself and grow into a pattern, one that would almost certainly repeat itself if you had the misfortune to encounter another abuser.

Let us not forget that there may already be another abuser in your life – a parent, a friend, a colleague or boss, almost anyone can exhibit abusive behavior. That doesn't mean you need to be that person's victim, even if you have been in the past.

You will also have heard the old cliché about people

28

who always end up going for the "wrong type" in their romantic lives. When it comes to abuse, that's absolutely possible; for instance, consider the symptom of loss of self. Thanks to your abuser, you lost the ability to make decisions about yourself and your future – it would seem only natural, if you are not fully healed from the experience, for you to seek a new partner who can make up for that lack, plummeting you straight back into the pattern of abuse.

How to identify what's not working in the relationship that is actually working for you.

When you have been in a relationship with a narcissist into the third phase, the longer you have been together, the more lost you can become.

For people who have become victims of a narcissistic personality, they feel the effects in many similar ways, yet it is always a personal experience. Some victims will only get psychologically abused, whereas some experience the entire gambit to include physical violence.

Most survivors would agree that they feel quite lost or even brainwashed. They also report that they felt as if the narcissist was a sort of energy vampire that would suck the life and hope out of a victim slowly but surely.

29

When victims are under the narcissist's spell, they start to have this mental filter that is a constant dialogue in their heads. They are constantly questioning what they think, say, or do and if it will be something that the narcissist will approve or not, or if it is something that will upset them. It creates an environment where they are second-guessing themselves to a point where it becomes a crippling effect overall.

Once the victim has gotten to the point of where the narcissist has brainwashed them up to the point where they do not even know who they are anymore, they will start to glance in the mirror and not recognize who is looking back either. It is hard to believe unless you have already gotten to this point.

This leads to a dissociation with their environment. They will start to experience continuous breaks in their sense of self, consciousness, perceptions, and memory. If this state is allowed to continue, the victim will start having numb emotions. This state is made worse if the narcissist is using drugs as a control tool, which further incapacitates their victim into waking up to the actual reality of what is occurring.

All the worries and actions of the victims revolve around the narcissist. Everything else that used to matter to them, including themselves, gets put on the back burner. The narcissist and their happiness and needs become the number one priority.

Trauma bonding is what occurs over a period of time, and this bond makes it rather difficult for the victim to leave the situation they so desperately hate. It is so incredibly easy for an outsider to simply tell them to leave, but it is not that easy. One reason for this is they have had all their hopes stripped away from them and that they do not see any options of escape. Another reason is that most victims have gotten into a state where they cannot trust themselves or anyone else, so they continue to feel helpless, trapped in the situation.

The victim may start having somatic symptoms which were not present before the relationship with the narcissist. These can present themselves in a plethora of ways including weight loss, stomach, autoimmune or reproductive system issues. This is due to the high-stress levels that are present, which makes your immune system weak, bringing on illnesses much more rapidly.

When a victim gets to the hopeless and crippling point, they are twice more likely to commit suicide on several occasions. This is the sad reality for many victims of narcissism as they see no other way out.

You might not realize at the beginning of the relationship that the fights that you have every once in a while, slowly start to build up. Over time, you start to realize that every fight ends with you being the one in the wrong.

This happens no matter what started the conversation, be it for simple respect or an apology that the narcissist must say. As the fight persists, you, the victim, are the one who ends up apologizing to the narcissist, as they skillfully turn the conversation around to their favor. Even when the narcissist has treated you in despicable ways, they are always the victim.

And with this scenario played over the next months and years, you start to believe in all the subtle manipulative comments, put-downs, and downright lies. This is not even a conscious effort as your brain and reasoning of thought have been slowly picked away.

In the end, you believe that no one could be in your company and enjoy themselves because you are completely worthless and a failure as a human being.

When the narcissist has used the manipulation technique of isolation on you, they have essentially used the same tactic as they commonly do in war times. They set up blockades to hinder free trade or people moving freely.

The blockades that the narcissist utilizes are emotional and mental blocks to barricade you against the rest of the world. This is to gain complete control of every aspect of your life, including your thoughts and actions. To further support the idea of isolation, the narcissist may start the physical abuse which further tears down the victim.

Once the isolation has been implemented successfully, the victim falls further under the rule of the narcissist and is taught to believe that there is no escape. This is their life, and they better behave the way the narcissist pleases at the time, or it will get worse. The narcissist, at this point, is teaching the victim learned helplessness to place puppet strings on the victim for the narcissist's pleasure.

In this state of mind, the victim gives up trying to resist because it no longer has any effect. The victim goes into survival mode. The reality of the victim's days usually caused them to get into drugs or alcohol to escape their current state of affairs as they slip deeper into a depressed state.

The longer you stay in this state of mind, the more your self-identity slips away. You become totally reliant on the narcissist and feel like you are unable to complete even the simplest of tasks that used to come so easily to you. This is a dangerous place to be because many victims consider suicide as an only option for escape.

You also may have suffered from a loss of self-identity. If the relationship with the narcissist was for a short period of time, there will be more of your identity left after the fact. However, the victims who were with the narcissist for years may lose their self-identity all together.

Because of the controlling nature of most narcissists, you may have been forced to miss out on opportunities to better yourself. This could have been through a job offer, furthering your education, or even traveling. This is another negative aspect which bonds you to the narcissist further because they are monopolizing your time to fully place it on them.

You may also be suffering from anxiety or depression due to the narcissist constantly cutting you down. This could be from them putting down your actions or appearances. The continued barrage of cut downs will lead to you believing these falsehoods. It also further has you rely on the narcissist because they make you believe that no one else would want you because you are simply not good enough.

You also feel very restless when you are alone. You constantly use any free time that you have to try to please the narcissist further. This could be trying to earn more money, buying them gifts, or even cleaning the house. You never spend any time doing anything that you enjoy because the narcissist has created an environment that focuses solely on their contentment. However, over time, you realize there is never any way to fully please a narcissist.

Take everything slowly

Making new changes in your life can be overwhelming. This is a new stage in your life – a new found freedom as it were. Sometimes you will find it hard to communicate with other people. For the first time in your life you are deciding something for yourself.

No one's there to tell you what to do and no one is telling you what you can or can't do. Take everything one step at a time. All of this is part of the huge healing process that you will have to go through.

If you were prevented from making new friends then start slowly. Find acquaintances in your neighborhood first. Try something that you haven't done before—but do one thing at a time. Try to find things that interest you.

35

Don't rush. If you rush things you might find yourself using toxic coping tools and that will not get you moving forward in life.

How to interrupt the same recurring painful patterns and why nothing ever seems to get resolved.

At some point, enough is enough. There are times when you just have to block and cut the narcissist out of your life. This is especially true of abusive relationships. If you need to get a court order to keep the narcissist out of your hair, then do it.

Note that sometimes keeping away from the narcissist's presence will feel uncomfortable. Some people have gotten so used to the feeling of being dominated that they feel that there is something missing without it.

It will take a while before that feeling goes away. Sometimes it's scary. But if you follow the tips and steps mentioned above, you will move on with your life. It's never easy, but the rewards will be worth it.

You can be forgiven for thinking that the narcissist cares about you because most humans have this innate desire to care about each other, and our default setting is to assume that others are also capable of caring about us. When you start out with the narcissist, he will give you the impression that he cares, but that is all an illusion because he wants something out of it. When the narcissist finally reveals his true colors, and you realize that he doesn't care, it can be a disconcerting experience, and you can even remain in denial about it for a very long time. That is because we are wired to look for the good in others, and when there is none to find, we keep digging deep. Don't waste your time that way once you figure out that someone is a narcissist. It's time for the assumption that he cares to go out of the window.

Remember that the narcissist is quite devious, and he/she can take advantage of the fact that you think there is some good in him/her by feigning it once in a while to keep you on the hook. For example, if you are married to a narcissist who spends the cash in your joint accounts on things that benefit only him/her and put you in a financial quagmire, if he/she figures out that you are growing weary and you are about to leave, he/she may decide to spend some of that money on a "gift" for you, just to get you thinking that maybe he/she isn't that bad.

An emotionally abusive narcissist may decide to buy you flowers once in awhile just to get you thinking that maybe all is not lost in that relationship. You have to remember that these are just tricks that are meant to manipulate you so that you can stick around and suffer more abuse. In the narcissist's mind, he/she probably thinks that the occasional decent act negates all the horrible things that he/she does to you. Don't be fooled by the occasional kind acts.

You might ask, if a narcissist doesn't care, then why does he/she give me so much attention? This is a very confusing thing, and it has led many people to excuse the behavior of the narcissists in their lives for a long time. The truth is that for narcissists, attention is about control, having power over you, and manipulating you. Tricking you into thinking they care about you is like a sport to them, and they have a lot of fun with it. It's a sick game that they play with you to gain your trust. Once you trust them, they are going to manipulate you and bring out your insecurities so that you are somewhat dependent on them for emotional stability.

The sooner you accept the fact that the narcissist doesn't care, the sooner you will be able to get out from under his/her control, and the sooner you will be able to start healing and rebuilding your self-esteem. The longer you are stuck thinking the narcissist cares, the harder it will be for you to free yourself from his/her influence. There are people who have tolerated narcissists for so long, to the point that they have become numb to their own suffering and they have accepted the abuse as part of their existence. Don't let the narcissist break you, and don't lose perspective — you know a caring person when you see one, so don't make excuses for the narcissist.

Don't Engage the Narcissist in Psychological Games

Narcissists are very good at initiating dramatic psychological games, often at your expense. They can stir up conflict between you and other people, and once you are at each other's throats, they'll pretend they had absolutely nothing to do with the situation at hand. So, if you sense that a narcissist is playing some sort of mind game with the intention of getting you to react in an aggressive way, you should take a step back.

Narcissists play games and start drama because they enjoy the chaos that ensues as a result of their machinations. When a narcissist starts a conflict between two people, he/she feels a sense of superiority over them — it feels like he/she is the puppet-master and you and others are tiny puppets ready to rip each other apart while he/she plays god over your lives. So, before you fall into the trap that the narcissist sets for you, and find yourself tangled in a drama whose origin you can't even remember, let's look at some of the common games that a narcissist may try to get you involved in.

One common game that narcissists play is the "emotional ping pong" game. This is where a person avoids taking responsibility for their actions by throwing that responsibility back to you. If the narcissist has done something reprehensible, instead of reflecting on his/her own actions and admitting wrongdoing, he/she will throw the ball back at you somehow. He/she could try to blame you, shame you, project fault onto you, or even outright deny doing something wrong, making you seem crazy for even pointing it out. If you care about him/her, you might find yourself believing the lie and even making excuses on his/her behalf.

Narcissists always love to play different variations of the 'game' where they make you seem crazy in front of other people. A narcissist could do something that indicates to you that they have malicious intent, but when you confront them, they can accuse you of having an overactive imagination, feigning innocence, or they can turn it around by accusing you of malice.

They could even get everyone around you to turn

against you by making outrageous public accusations. Once you fall into that trap, you will start spinning out of control trying to prove to others that you are right, but that will only serve to prove the narcissist right. You have to learn to avoid reacting dramatically to the actions of a narcissist, and you have to be able to tell when you are being set up (with a narcissist, always assume that he/she is setting you up for something).

Don't engage in the narcissist's drama. Don't play games. As a decent person, you will be inhibited by your rationality and your sense of decency. The narcissist won't play by any rules, so you can be absolutely certain that you will lose. The best way to win with a narcissist is to avoid playing his/her games altogether.

Detach with Love

Detaching with love is a term that has been used by experts to mean that you are cutting off a person in a relationship minus, the resentment. You are letting go, but not because you hate that person. Yes, you can let go of a narcissist without hating them.

And detaching with love gives you a chance for closure—at least on your side of the bargain. The narcissist may not be willing to let go or even forgive.

41

But you're doing it anyway, not because you no longer want to care, but because it is no longer your business.

The first step to detaching with love is to accept and realize that there is nothing at this point that you can do to help your narcissist. There is no longer any way you can fix mom.

It is time to accept the fact that you can't help your narcissist no matter how hard you try. And now it is time to let go. There is no need for you to step in, it is time for the narcissist to take responsibility for his or her actions.

That way, they are learning to do something for themselves and you are now on your way to recovery and healing. It's the perfect win/win for both of you.

How to Deal with Narcissistic Rage at The Narcissists Life

- Do not respond to the rage. It will only make things escalate from there. You will never win the argument no matter what facts you have on your side. It doesn't matter.

- Do not believe that whatever you tell this person that it will change their mind. It won't happen.

- Do not use logic or reason when pleading your case. It will only make it last longer. Your opinion does not matter.

- Learn to be calm. Easier said than done, obviously, but so necessary. This is for your own good. Use centering techniques such as meditation and mindfulness to help calm your mind down. The more you get used to it, the better you will be able to handle the rage when it comes.

- Do not overreact to the rage. He or she wants just that. They are itching for a fight and want to engage. It keeps you firmly in control of the narrative as well. This is important for after the rage passes. They won't admit fault but will not have something to throw back in your face later.

- Agree with them for the moment. Call it placating, call it whatever, it doesn't matter. You are doing what you need to do to get through the fight in one piece. Also, use tact when you back off. Do not make it seem like you are simply indulging them. The discussion of issues can come up later when the dust has settled. Practice doing something the narcissist is incapable of, empathy. Place yourself in their shoes. It could prove to be a valuable weapon in your arsenal.

- Create distance. If you need to leave the room, go. If you need to spend the night at a friend's, do it. Time apart is important and it will give the rage a chance to pass without further damage being inflicted.

- Speak in an even tone. Keep things under control and do not threaten him or her or challenge their supposed authority,at least for the time being.

- Time to think. Ask if it is ok to think about what has been said so that an acceptable solution can be found.

- Remember, it isn't about you. The narcissist has certain perceptions that are skewed and can't help it. It is not about what you did or did not do. Keeping that perspective will help you accomplish the other things on this list in a much easier way.

Getting Back in the Driver's Seat

Once you realize who you are dealing with, there are some measures to take to ensure your overall mental and physical health. You must learn to practice being more assertive which will make you more confident in your dealings with the narcissist in your life.

Because NPD personalities are rather difficult to keep a healthy relationship with, it may be wise to keep some distance from them when possible. Sometimes this is not wholly possible. In this case, be sure to set your boundaries when you are in their presence. Recognize when control and manipulation tactics are being used and be detached by not reacting.

To keep the narcissist from retaliating in such a grand scale, practice less confrontational methods to communicate. Be sure to do this in a one on one scenario or with a friend present. Large crowds will backfire on you as the narcissist will feel more threatened.

If you realize that they are never going to change and let go of any expectation of this happening, this will be a better mindset in the long run. They will only change if they choose to after getting to the point of hitting rock bottom.

Make solid personal goals and plan them to the finest detail with proposed dates. When you have something to focus on, you will notice when you are driven off course much more easily. This will reduce the amount of successful manipulation that can continue to take place.

Be sure to keep a paper trail for the events that need remembering, be it for your own personal growth or the authorities. Unless you have laws that allow you to record conversations, refrain from doing so.

Try to remain detached and let anything that the manipulator does just roll off your back. It may get rather difficult to accomplish this as the narcissist may become quite brutal in their attacks. Keep the right perspective. Everything that they do is potential evidence to use in your favor later.

Keep the knowledge that you are dealing with a narcissist close to your chest, and this will be more beneficial as you will know the tell-tale signs of control and manipulation techniques. You will be more aware of how not to get wrapped into the narcissist's trap.

If you feel like you are being manipulated into a decision, allow yourself to be able to sleep on the idea. If it is honest, it will still be available for that short period of time. This will also allow you to be able to think thoroughly about the situation before you commit yourself, and minimize the chance of being manipulated into something you really do not want to do.

Sometimes the best reaction is no reaction at all. If you feel like a narcissist is being insincere or being manipulative, it would be best to walk away from the situation without getting emotional. Remember that the narcissist is looking for an emotional reaction from you. If you are not willing to play their game, they will eventually not want to play either as they will find another person for an outlet.

It is best to refrain from calling out the narcissist for their lies and who they truly are. The backlash from this action would be narcissistic injury of which the narcissist will lash out in anger or in ways that are detrimental mentally, physically or psychologically to the person. With the common lack of morals or emotions, narcissists can certainly be some of the most vindictive group of people you will come across.

If you are not able to get away from the narcissist in your life, you may end up needing to just kiss up to them and flatter them. This is what they are looking for in the long run, and as long as you are aware of who you are dealing with, you should be able to keep a healthy distance from getting roped into the narcissist trap. You do not have to go overboard with this task.

It would be best to give a healthy dose of attention to these people and make yourself busy otherwise. You must realize that anything that the narcissist does is not personal as they treat all of the victims that they catch in the same exact way. Even when it comes to loyalty, they are unable to **not** cheat on their primary partner.

Chapter 3:
Assert credibility

Was It Really an Abusive Relationship?

O ne of the common hurdles we face in the final days of an abusive relationship and the immediate aftermath is acceptance. Was this really the abusive situation it suddenly seems, or am I overreacting? Could this possibly have happened to me? Could this person I loved so deeply and for so long really be the monster it now seems they are?

Even after you walk away, this feeling often persists. Did I just make a mistake? Am I being unfair? Should I give them another chance? It comes from the deepest parts of your heart, fuelled by the love that first cemented your attachment to your abuser.

That, you see, is why an emotionally abusive relationship can be so disastrous. Love is a positive emotion, a bond that ties parent to child, sibling to sibling, friend to friend and, of course, lover to lover. It's a beautiful, wonderful part of the human experience, which makes it all the crueler for your abuser to have used it against you.

49

Every abusive relationship is different, but there is still an overall range of symptoms. In your moment of realization, you saw at least one of them, maybe more. To take on the mantle of survivor – a crown you have very much owned – you will need to accept what happened to you. Take a look through this list and see how many of them apply to your situation. Even one or two can be enough to pin the definition of abuse onto your relationship.

- Your partner was adept at manipulating you into doing things their way. They knew the right words to say, the right strings to pull and the right emotions to tap to make you do what they wanted you to do.

- On the flipside, your partner was seldom interested in your needs or desires and usually squashed them at the very moment you made them known – unless there was something in it for themselves. This can sometimes be a difficult one to spot because abusers can be adept at giving you just enough hope and happiness to keep you blind to what's really going on.

- Your partner was involved in every life decision you made, hovering in the corner of your eye, influencing your choices to make sure you stayed on the path they preferred. This was true from the littlest of decisions to the biggest – you felt as though they were inside your mind along with you, altering your destiny, though at the time it likely felt more akin to "help" than manipulation.

- You were seldom the one choosing the direction of your relationship. Your partner chose vacation destinations, weekend activities, even how the chores were divided between you. Their manipulation made this feel perfectly normal.

- You were expected to be and act a certain way to meet the expectations of your partner. Meeting those standards was exhausting and most of the time you felt you were falling short, which pushed you to try even harder to please them.

- The relationship was unpredictable, like walking on eggshells. You were

51

emotionally exhausted a lot of the time from trying to predict what your partner wanted, and then fulfill it before they became angry, accusing or "disappointed" with you. You wanted to make them happy and you wanted to build a loving and lasting relationship, so this constant chaos spurred you to work tirelessly to make that happen.

- You have changed in countless small ways from the person you were before. From the way you dress to the way you act in social settings, your partner slowly molded you into the person they wanted. Your partner made you doubt your own memory, your own conclusions about things, even your sanity itself. They did this through lies, misdirection, contradiction, denials and more, leaving you dizzy and disoriented. It's known as "gaslighting", and the world is only recently waking up to how often it happens.

- Your partner damaged your self esteem and confidence, needling at you constantly. They criticized you, made you feel small, told you off like a child when you acted in a way they didn't approve of and made you feel that everything was your fault – and never theirs.

- You have been separated from most of the friends and family you cherish. Slowly, over time, you stopped spending as much time with them because your partner was working to isolate you – some, they may have even convinced you to cut out of your life entirely.

- Your partner often used emotional blackmail to get their own way, using your guilt or fear or even your love for them to get their own way.

- Your partner insisted on sexual contact you didn't really want, telling you that you would sleep with them if you really loved them, complaining you weren't fulfilling their needs.

A lot of these behaviors are pretty normal, taken on their own. Even in the healthiest of relationships, there is sometimes turmoil, there are arguments and criticisms. Most of us, at least sometimes, want to get our own way.

It's because we can excuse these acts individually that we often dismiss the bigger picture. We tell ourselves that we're imagining it, that it's our own fault or that it's just a bad phase. Sometimes, we don't tell ourselves anything at all – we simply accept.

Don't Second-Guess Your Decisions When Dealing with a Narcissist

You don't need to justify yourself to the narcissist. When you interact with a narcissist, he/she will insist that you explain certain actions and choices that you have taken. You have to remember that your decisions are in your own best interests, and you don't owe the narcissist any explanation. Once you bother to explain yourself to the narcissist, it opens the door for him/her to then plant the seed of doubt on the decision that you have made with the intention of making you second guess yourself so that they can regain control over you. By all means, don't explain yourself. Let them know that you have already made a decision and that you are not seeking their input on the matter. It may seem rude, but it's necessary.

You can be certain that the narcissists will keep pushing for you to explain things to them. As we have mentioned in the last chapter, the only way to win a narcissist's game is to avoid playing it altogether. The narcissist will go out of his/her way to make you think that they are just trying to help, or that they are just making friendly conversation, but once you take the bait and offer an explanation for an action you have taken or a decision you have made, the narcissist will come up with a hundred different questions and observations, all of which are tailor-made to diminish your conviction. He/she will tell you it's not in your best interest to do what you are doing, you are not smart enough or strong enough to do it, or you need their help to see your plan through.

The narcissist knows that when you start doubting your perceptions and your convictions, you will have to rely on his/her guidance a lot more and that will give him/her control over you. When you get to the point where you don't trust your own judgment, then you will accept the narcissist's judgment, and he/she will be able to tell you what to do, and how to think and act at all times.

First, the narcissist will start by telling a blatant lie. Since this is a person that you have known for a while and you trust to some level, the lie will throw you off balance, and you will start doubting things that are obvious. Next, the narcissist will deny things that they said, even if you can prove that they did. The more vehement their denial, the more you question your own reality!

The narcissist succeeds in gaslighting you because he/she wears you down over time. It's easy to think that you are too smart to get gaslighted, but the fact is that it doesn't happen instantaneously, it happens gradually, and one day you will wake up and find that you are so far gone. The way it works is that the narcissist will tell a small lie, stick with it and make you question your reality a little bit, but then you will decide that it's too small a lie to matter, so you will let it slide. The lies will then escalate both in magnitude and in frequency, and since you let the first one slide, you will have an easy time doing the same with the subsequent lies, until you get to the point where it's a norm. So, you shouldn't second guess yourself or let an obvious lie slide for even a second. Don't let the narcissist desensitize you to his/her lies.

Narcissists have perfected the art of turning things around to make it sound like you were the selfish one when it's clear that they are taking advantage of you. While you are still confused trying to decipher what it is that they are doing, they will make great strides towards altering your whole reality.

They will also send confusing signals by occasionally acknowledging some of your claims so that you begin to think that perhaps you were mistaken about the rest of the claims.

Is There a Future for a Relationship Touched by Narcissism?

What one person is happy to put up with, another person would run away from. What you need to do, however, is ask yourself whether you're truly happy and whether you see a future for the two of you. Never stick with a narcissistic person if they are making you feel unhappy, belittled, or questioning your own self-esteem or sanity.

Many men and women stay in narcissistic relationships because they aren't sure whether or not they're imagining it, or whether it's really happening. Whenever their partner shows their bad side, they quickly show their good side not long afterwards; by doing that, they're keeping the person right where they want them - not leaving.

In terms of whether there is a future or not, perhaps we should instead be questioning whether there is a healthy future or not. There is a difference between a general future and a healthy one. A relationship where one partner is constantly belittling and dragging down another isn't healthy, whether they're doing it because of a personality disorder or not.

There aren't that many narcissists who remain in relationships for that long. The reason is that in the end, the other partner really sees the light and finds the strength to leave. This doesn't always happen, and there are instances where a future could be in the cards, provided the narcissistic partner is able to realize what they are doing and get help. It does happen, but it doesn't happen often.

Whilst we might be painting a bleak picture, it really is a case of looking at your individual circumstances and deciding what is right for you. There is no right or wrong answer here.

Can the Narcissist Change?

For most of us with healthy empathetic capacities, shame works as an uncomfortable but necessary motivator. It's important to note that shame isn't the same as embarrassment or humiliation, which is when shame is thrust upon you through the opinions and reactions of others; shame, by contrast, usually comes from within, as a sense that any humiliation or embarrassment experienced is justified and deserved. When we do something that is morally reprehensible, we feel guilt and shame in our physical bodies; these emotions can cause stomach upset, headaches, shortness of breath, even vision or speech problems in extreme cases. These sensations are unpleasant because they have to be in order to inspire us to change, grow, and make wiser, healthier choices in the future.

Of course, an excess of shame can become hard-wired into the brain through long-term exposure to narcissistic regimes. Narcissists are a different story, though. They are masters at escaping their own shame, constantly pawning it off on their victims. Therefore, they rarely experience the discomfort of shame, and they are unlikely to ever feel inspired to change or seek out help.

Without ever having to face or process their guilt, they most often feel light and airy, empowered, and carefree, so long as they never feel their superiority is being threatened. Therapy will likely seem like a waste of money and time to them; they are happy with their lifestyles and believe that people who bother to struggle with processing their own negative emotions are mostly chumps.

The only time it is reasonable to expect a narcissist to change is if you note a true effort on their part to engage in self-reflection. If their way of life isn't working out for them, they may be personally inspired to question their behavior patterns, regardless of external impetus to do so. This is a rare scenario, but it certainly isn't beyond the realm of possibility. There are some, though, who would argue that this thought process implies a severe infestation of fleas, rather than an actual personality disorder.

Ultimately, in order for a narcissist to heal and change, they'll have to grow comfortable with accepting responsibility for their own actions. Since they are well practiced at avoiding such responsibility and are generally only motivated to do things which benefit them, they would have to be inspired to change as a way to improve their lives and feel better. The difficult practice of self-reflection may need to be framed as a means to a glorious end in order for a narcissist to even consider engaging meaningfully.

Most narcissists that seek therapy are often brought to the realization that they need help by someone close to them, such as a parent or spouse or close friend. There needs to be a genuine actualization within them that has shed light on the consequences of their narcissism to those around them and indeed on themselves. They need a push, a shove, and a kick in order to seek help - their stubbornness or lack of acknowledging their narcissism can often get in the way of this and impair their ability, or rather their newly-acquired need for help. Narcissists need to feel a sense of fear, something that will affect them negatively if they do not seek help, such as their loved one leaving them or, if you're their employer, fired from their job.

A narcissist can get help through therapeutic approaches, such as schema therapy (the process whereby the narcissist revisits past events where an alternative response could have been made and positively affected that respective situation and allows the narcissist to go back and rewrite that part of their life through revealing their true, vulnerable self), or by seeking help through a therapist. A therapist offers a base for the narcissist to talk openly and the therapist, in turn, should be invulnerable to the charismatic ways of the narcissist.

Therapy in itself does not imply that the narcissist is alone in these sessions; his or her partner could also be seeking help in ways to deal with the narcissistic partner while actively looking for ways in which to better and strengthen their relationship.

With this said, though some narcissists are willing to change, most are not. Why? Because, upon the layer of "nostalgia", lies a deep, deep deniability to doing anything wrong or to behaving in an off-emotional manner towards people. They are incapable of admitting to this. Though, in certain situations, they are able to see that change is needed when they have done something that, even to them, has crossed a line. They realize that their behavior has become mentally unavoidable and they make the decision to take steps forward through therapy.

Chapter 4:
Show them the benefits

Acknowledgment

When we are dealing with a narcissist whose opinion seems to be the only one that "should be taken into account," we can simply acknowledge the narcissist, thank them for their opinion, and then to make sure that we have made certain that they seem sure that we appreciate their opinion. We can thank them and do whatever we want with that information. By acknowledging the narcissist's opinion, we have navigated a safer route around the definite feeling of scorn that would have otherwise been directed towards us by the narcissist. By doing this we have been the "adult" in the situation and have seemingly heightened the narcissist's self-esteem by making them think that we **will** use their advice and suggestions, even though to a degree we will not be taking it into consideration. Avoiding the conflict which comes from challenging the narcissist's opinion allows us to show an interest in what the narcissist has said.

<u>Understanding</u>

While acknowledging a narcissist implies that we listen and do not take their comments into consideration; understanding the narcissist means we are actually listening to them and taking into account what they have said. Understanding is a little bit more complex. Though this tactic can usually save us from the wrath of the narcissist, understanding their opinion takes a little more nous. We need to make sure that we let them know that we value them, and then listen to what they have said, keenly listening until, from underneath all that self-absorbed theory, we can piece together our own picture of what they have said. This can be entirely frustrating, but it is something that we should do sometimes. Behind their mask is someone who has gotten to the top quickly, despite stepping on everyone to get there. Often, when we dissect what they have said and omitted the spotlight fever connotations, we can actually get a clear picture of what they are talking about, thus meaning that the advice they have given can actually be applied to a certain situation in which we are going through. For instance, when someone with NPD explains their success in such detail, as they usually do, we hear bits and pieces of information which makes us think,

"Hang on a minute. That is actually quite sound advice." Yes, the underlying argument is how they are so successful or how they did some amazing thing over the weekend, but somewhere in that mix is something useful. Understanding the narcissist is a heat-deflector and grudge-deflator.

Staying Calm

If you are not a person who can easily deal with a narcissist, then staying calm is by far the most difficult practice for you when they start going on about this and that. It irks you, creates this massive bubble of steaming water that wants to spill over. We all have been there, don't worry. It is that feeling when what they have said is so mean or just dumbfounding that we ball up our fists, sigh, smile, and nod our heads; that frustration that is about to explode; the emotion of complete and utter anger that fills us and consumes us. But we can deal with that emotion. It takes time to perfect it, but staying calm, especially when the narcissist you are around is persistent in his or her presentation of themselves, can be a life-changing tool in being at peace with the situation or interaction. Sure, it is extremely difficult, but accepting that situation or interaction with the narcissist and then finding a small piece of calm within you can certainly go a long way. For instance, a narcissist starts explaining all that you did wrong, whether this narcissist is someone at work or your loved one, and you become awash with anger, but know how the narcissist will react. Do you shout and go off and get nowhere with the narcissist or do you try your best to stay calm, listen, and then just move on? Everybody snaps eventually and that is our human nature, our survival instincts kicking in. It is a normal reaction. It is the pressure building up and our tempers becoming unhinged. But, we do need to be aware that by arguing with or retorting back at a narcissist only affects you and not them.

Try Not to Take the Narcissist's Actions Personally

To the narcissist, it's never actually about you. To him or her, you are a pawn in a mind game that they are playing, and if you weren't there, they would be doing the exact same thing to someone else. Of course, this doesn't make their abuse less painful, but at least it clarifies things for you. It means that your suffering isn't a result of any wrongdoing on your part.

When your relationship or your association with a narcissist finally goes south (as it is bound to do), you are going to start wondering how this person that you have known and trusted could have morphed into an entirely different and means a person who you don't recognize at all. You will start thinking that maybe you did something to deserve their anger and their animosity. In your mind, you will feel that there has to be a rational explanation for what has happened. There is, of course, a psychological explanation for the things that are happening — but you can rest assured that you didn't play a part in making those things happen. They were just meant to happen, and they were never truly within your control.

The narcissist isn't hurting you or targeting you for a personal reason. You have nothing to do with it. The narcissist acts the way he/she does because that is the nature of the beast. It may seem callous, but it's true. The narcissist targeted you because you just happened to cross his/her path, or you just happened to be in their life.

If you have a narcissistic parent, you will realize that he/she treats both you and your siblings with the same level of narcissism (it may vary at different times, but everyone gets their share of abuse over the years). If you are in a relationship with a narcissist, you can be certain that he/she treated his/her former lovers the same way. In other words, the narcissist is

67

an equal opportunity torturer.

This information doesn't make the suffering that you endured under the narcissist any less painful, but it has several important implications for you. First, it means that there is nothing wrong with you and that there is nothing that you did to deserve what the narcissist has done to you. Many people take the abuse of narcissists because they get accustomed to the suffering, and they start internalizing the idea that they might have done something to set off the abuse. Most narcissists will try to blame you for lots of things, so if you let them, they can easily convince you that you have done something to deserve the suffering.

The second implication here is that there is absolutely nothing that you could have done to control the actions of the narcissists because those are his/her natural tendencies. Many people stay in abusive relationships with narcissists because they harbor the false belief that they can change them. Now that you know the narcissist's actions aren't personal, you understand that there is no way you can control those actions, so it's futile to believe that you can change a narcissist. That should clear your conscience and make it easy for you to end the relationship or the association with the narcissist (if you can).

The third implication is that the failure of your relationship with a narcissist isn't a commentary on your ability to give or receive love (the relationship was doomed to fail from the very beginning). So, as you leave, and as you move on, you shouldn't carry the baggage from that relationship onto the next one. The only thing you should bring along with you is your newfound ability to spot a narcissist from a mile away.

Don't delude yourself into thinking that the narcissist actually cares about you because what's happening is completely and utterly impersonal. We have mentioned that some narcissists are seducers, and they can make you feel like you are the center of the universe when they are looking to manipulate you. When this happens, it can be very tempting to ignore your instincts and everything you have learned so far about narcissists, but you have to stay strong and retain your rationality.

What you should do if "he needs to change" but seems to be fine with mediocrity.

A narcissist needs to want to change. There needs to

be that moment in which they realize that they have done wrong. However, the decision to change needs to be true to the narcissist's personality: centered solely on them. The decision to change needs to be one that is such that it makes the narcissist feel almost compelled to seek help because of that compulsive inhibition that we call "drive". The people who are deeply involved in the life of the narcissist need to know that they cannot simply guilt the narcissist into changing; that does not work and it becomes more and more frustrating for the person involved when what they are pleading goes straight over the narcissistic person's head. You will feel hurt by this. However, as mentioned, the decision is solely the narcissist's decision. Expecting a narcissist to change will not benefit anybody. The realization that change is needed needs to be selfish and backed by that motivation and ambition to change for the better - they need to want to change for themselves by themselves. This can often create an atmosphere of enraged betrayal within the narcissist that you want them to change; remember, they are the ones who always want you to change. Their defensive mechanisms whir and spin out of control and you have lost the battle with them before it has even begun.

A narcissist is a lone wolf and they view change as unnecessary, or maybe even a little bit stupid, due to the image they have portrayed of themselves in their heads. And this can be said to be a pattern that is continuously played out through habitual idealization. These are just patterns in behavior that become their identity which the narcissist identifies themselves with; and with this, because they are a part of these patterns, they automatically shift erratic and harsh traits and incorporate them, until this behavior is a deep part of their personality.

Trying to change a narcissist does not work, as we know, without them seeing the need to change. Trying to plead with them to change is only going to exert more energy from you and leave you more confused and more upset. A narcissist simply does not know that they are acting in a negative manner or exhibiting negative behavior, and telling them that they are will only fall upon deaf ears. They do not see the desire to change because they feel their uniqueness and special, god-like existence is reason enough not to change. And they won't.

This can often leave you frustrated, but we need to remember that a narcissist was just born that way or raised in a way that made them that way. If there is no reason that stimulates the motivation and desire to change, they will continue as they are.

Behavioral Changes & Consequences

A narcissist can only change when they understand the consequences of their reactions and responses and know that they have crossed the line. A narcissist needs to open up in order to feel the consequences of their reactions. With that said, it needs to be felt emotionally for the effect of those consequences to be realized. Bluntly, the narcissist doesn't really understand why you feel that they need to change and subsequently do not listen to your qualms about them. They believe they are flawless and faultless and because of the distress, confusion and false praise they may have gone through or gotten during childhood, has created this protective shield which enshrouds them and encases them in a type false emotional identity. This is a consequence of upbringing. This is fact. But what we can also look at is the level at which a narcissist feels pain. Often, despite being sensitive underneath, they are immune emotionally to feelings, concerns, complaints, accusations, and finger-pointing.

The negative behavior that was externalized by physical infliction on someone else could have been the wake-up call that they needed in order to realize and then open themselves up to the realm of possible change.

The narcissist needs to be steadfast in his or her dedication to take the step forward to change and embrace that change. They need to believe they need to change. The feeling to change their negative or abusive behavior can be fleeting so it must be acted on. Narcissism is a medical disorder and it is easy for us to forget that the people it affects have been that way for many, many years and will inevitably struggle in their cause. However, with the correct help, suitable to them, change can take place. Baby steps. It is important for us - as those involved with the narcissist - that every step in the right direction is a small win in which they should be praised with such subtlety. Even though narcissists are over-confident individuals, when they are actively making an effort to change, we should embrace this and be with them to show them that we appreciate their hard and exhausting work.

A narcissist who is trying to change should be willing to look at their characteristics – be it their emotional responses, reactions, things they say, or how they act. This is where decision-making comes in and it is such an important part in finding that change they want to go through and experience. However, when conducting interviews with a few narcissists who did change for the better, they mentioned the anxiety that they felt, and the pressure of trying to change who they are.

For people with narcissism, there are many decisions to make; problems to be solved, which possible outcome is best for them, and how it affects them. This type of decision-making can cause high levels of stress and unnecessary pressure based on making whatever decision that you have to make. This - it can be said - causes anxiety or anxious behavior and can be quite harmful to the person. Sometimes making decisions has the ability to tire an individual to the point of exhaustion, such is the power of thought and the gripping stress over them. It is difficult and it is hard, and some anxiety that comes from decision-making can either be rational - clear short-term to long-term solution - or irrational - hastily-made short-term solution that can have adverse effects on the long-term perspectives, relationships, and well-being of the individual suffering from narcissism.

Regaining Self-Control

Self-control is a key factor in maintaining a clear

state of mind, and a narcissistic person needs to be able to utilize it when they are trying to change their behavior.

Having self-control if you are a narcissist is as paramount as any success that you can have. Often, their inhibitions can have negative aspects to them, and if they are in a state of emotional turmoil and thinking irrationally, they can lose all self-control, change back, and succumb to these negative inhibitions that they may have harbored deep within them.

Regaining self-control is often difficult to do but it is not impossible to do. We all go through times where we lose it a bit and need to somehow cool down, cool off, realign our minds and become our old selves again. The best way to do this is to find something that can calm you down; this could be a hobby, a hike, anything that relates and touches you in a way that it can allow you to immerse yourself into that form of relaxation and switch off. Regaining self-control needs serious tact, a quick change of direction, and the ability to stop in times of aggressively-charged or emotionally-charged behavior towards something or someone. Stopping, as an ideology in narcissism, may be insanely difficult to do; when they are enraged by something or someone they feel this animated pull of gravity, centering themselves - anchoring - to this one situation and become so infallibly blinded that they become, furthermore, a part of their narcissism and cannot see anything clearly. Narcissists see in singular paradigms, but those that are changing themselves emotionally can start seeing other emotion, other peoples' emotion.

By regaining self-control, a narcissist can effectively stop when things pull them so far down that there doesn't seem like there is any way back up. By stopping, they allow themselves choices; choices to stabilize, realign, refocus, see and realize how they affect people. This in part can bring them up to the surface of clarified thinking; the way in which they will be able to see the world and people in both the singular format and from the peripheral point-of-view.

How to communicate with a narcissist

The hardest task of being in a relationship with a narcissist is possibly communicating with them and telling them what you need or want. Their illness stops them from compromising and fuels them to always find ways to win. If you are going to break up or divorce a narcissist, expect it to be even more difficult than usual.

Narcissists live on the reactions of their victims. They enjoy watching their victims stress out on whatever they say or do. This makes it a must for victims to be educated about dealing with narcissists, so they can empower themselves and heal over time. You might eventually see how pitiful these narcissists are behind their scathing words and angst.

If you are in the process of breaking free from the claws of a narcissist, the safest thing for you to do is not to engage them. It is useless arguing with them when all the arguments thrown back and forth will conclude in favor of him or her.

For those who need to co-exist as parents, zero engagement may not be possible. However, it helps if you limit your communication and showcase of emotions when dealing with the narcissist. Don't tire yourself out by trying to reason with an unreasonable, narcissistic person.

The Narcissist's Awareness

Narcissists are notoriously stubborn and difficult to get through to. Their lack of empathy and grandiose behaviors can make it hard for them to really understand the wider impact of their behaviors beyond just getting what they want when they want it. Sometimes, through raising the narcissist's awareness of what she is doing and how it is causing problems, you can begin to improve their behaviors. Rarely, they will be willing to improve themselves, especially if they are relatively low in narcissistic traits, or they are borderline narcissistic but do not have a diagnosis. Those who are more narcissistic by nature will likely be much more disagreeable about the process and less willing to even entertain the idea that they are not perfect exactly the way they are. Remember, narcissists typically lack normal self-awareness and see the world through a distorted lens. It will take plenty of patience to raise the narcissist's awareness, and if you feel like it is too much for you, there is no shame in saying you cannot handle it.

Willing Interactions

For those few narcissists who are willing to improve themselves or recognize their shortcomings, discussions of problematic behavior can be quite useful. Just as you would take a child aside to discuss why it is not okay to behave a certain way, you can also tactfully discuss why something the narcissist is doing is more hurtful. Remember, narcissists have fragile egos, so tact is of the utmost importance.

For example, if the narcissist has a tendency to seek perfection and you suspect a schema of unrelenting standards, you may look for ways that you notice the narcissist succeeding and comment on them. When you notice the narcissist begin to nitpick at himself or other people, pointing out flaws, it could be acceptable to gently remind the narcissist that small flaws will not be a problem. Point out that perfection, while a fantastic concept, is rarely ever a goal that is productive, and comment on how you have noticed how harsh he is on himself and others. Identify that no one is really comfortable with the insistence of flawless and that his expectations make it difficult to work. By identifying the problem you and your coworkers may have, you have provided some awareness to the narcissist, so he recognizes that part of his behavior is problematic. By providing him with praise, you may challenge one of his schema's rules. This sort of conversation repeated over time can be beneficial to the narcissist, and may even ultimately challenge the schema enough for him to relent, even if only a little.

By pointing out his unwarranted harshness toward himself, you begin to plant the seed of the idea that perfection is not necessary. He may have developed these unrelenting standards due to a childhood of strict adherence to perfection, and could have been punished unfairly when they were not met. It is important to remember to treat the narcissist with the same grace you would use for a child still learning how to interact with the world. Do not feel discouraged or irritated if you have to continue to gently guide the narcissist toward the idea that less than perfect can still be successful.

It can also be useful to discuss with the narcissist that his actions can make him come across as harsh, or make people prefer to avoid him. This hangs another carrot in front of the narcissist: Attention. Narcissists crave positive attention and admiration, so the idea that being a little less unrelenting may bring more of that attention could be a fantastic motivator.

Unknowing Interactions

More often than not, the narcissist is not open to consciously correcting their behavior. True to their diagnosis, they are unwilling or unable to acknowledge that they may have any sort of a problem. If you were to approach them and say that something they are doing is a problem, they would likely explode at you, unleashing their narcissistic rage at you because you have just become a challenge to their distorted worldview. It is easier to chase you away than to accept that their view is flawed. With these people, much more tact is necessary.

Much like how you noticed the narcissist's unrelenting standards in the previous section, you should also look for the unwilling narcissist's schemas. Perhaps they have a tendency to distrust others, and because of that distrust, they are quick to accuse others around them as the problem, and constantly sabotaging relationships because they would rather be alone than vulnerable to others. This makes them especially difficult to work with, and you often find yourself unhappy when work requires you to interact with them.

Rather than accepting the narcissist's haughty attitude, you can use their distrustful nature to your advantage; always follow through with what you offer to do, even if it is met with ungratefulness. If you offer to bring them a coffee, follow through with it, even if they accuse you of doing it to get them to do more of the work. They are distrustful of you because you have not given them a reason to trust you. If you offer to go over their paperwork to check for errors before submitting a group project for work, do it and make sure to sandwich any criticism between praises of things that are working well in the project. This not only lessens the blow to their ego, but makes them feel less like you are intentionally trying to hurt them when you have more compliments than criticisms.

No matter what, you need to avoid affirming their rule of avoiding trusting people. Even when it is difficult, it is imperative that you try your hardest to follow through with everything you say you will do. Even if you have been making good progress, a single slip up could send all of that progress down the drain.

Over time, through plenty of diligence and working with the narcissist's traits instead of being offended and affirming the maladaptive schemas, you will begin to tear the schemas down. Eventually, they may recognize that you are not out to get them and are genuinely trying to help. When the narcissist is unwilling to admit fault, it is important to let the narcissist arrive at that conclusion without you saying it, making it their decision rather than them feeling as if they are bowing down to someone else.

Care and Practice

Ultimately, when trying to raise a narcissist's awareness of his disordered behavior, you must learn their schemas to the best of your ability and take special care to control the triggers that make the narcissist feel a need to act upon their schemas. Their schemas are poor attempts at coping with stress and discomfort, and remembering that can help you remember to have the compassion and understanding that the narcissist is not necessarily trying to hurt you, but is acting true to his nature. Understanding the narcissist's core self and recognizing it as their attempt to control the world to protect himself can help you remember that it is important to avoid known triggers if it is practical or reasonable. Think of this as knowing not to poke the sleeping bear, no matter how tempting it may be.

While you should never goad the narcissist into known behaviors by using their known triggers, you should also never force yourself to walk on eggshells around them. If the only reasonable answer to a situation is something that may trigger the narcissist, then that is understandable. Do your best to control the triggers, but do not dedicate your life to constantly placating the narcissist, as this will only feed into their sense of entitlement.

While taking care to avoid triggers when possible, you should also practice techniques that help establish a healthy relationship and create positive interactions between yourself and the narcissist. As discussed earlier, remember that working with the narcissist's schemas can help you begin to develop a more meaningful relationship built upon trust that you will not hurt them the way they have been hurt in the past. They may begin to recognize that you are there as support rather than as another adversary wanting to tear them down, and you may find their behavior becoming healthier and more productive as they have less and less reason to use their maladaptive schemas to cope with stress.

How to have compassion for a narcissist

It may not be easy to feel compassion for a person who has bullied you, abused you, and treated you like dirt, but narcissists still need compassion. Granted, they may use it against you if you are not careful, but your loved ones who happen to be narcissists will need all the support that they can get as they try to live with their disorder.

Narcissists may have an idea that what they are doing isn't right, but their lack of empathy won't let them do anything about it. They might not even fully understand the impacts of their negative behaviors. They would not know how to spot the problem, let alone, solve it, because they know that they do not exist to cater to the world, but it is the other way around. Compassion for their dilemma, by understanding the origin of their real negative behavior, can help you get through life with them.

While you are struggling with feeling compassion for a narcissistic person, don't forget about showing compassion for yourself. You are the one suffering the most right now. You might feel frustrated about not being able to do enough and about all the mistakes that you committed in the past. Feel that compassion for yourself by acknowledging the fact that you lived in a world where the narcissist was the center of everything.

Even narcissists need compassion because not all of them are monsters or behaving like one. You may try to heal your emotional pain by detaching yourself emotionally from the narcissist in your life. However, this does not mean that you can ignore that person. How are you any different from narcissists if you continue to ignore them? Remember all the good things that the person did for you to make it easier to feel compassion towards them.

What to expect from a narcissist?

Dealing with a narcissistic spouse or partner means

that every day could be a challenge. However, it helps if you know what to expect from them, so you won't end up disappointed.

A narcissistic spouse does not have any respect for you and your marriage. They might even encourage talks against you, gossip about you, and fool you into believing that he or she is in love with you.

Promises are actually made to be broken, all the time. Narcissists make them, but will likely not honor them. When you confront them about it, they will vehemently deny it. They might even feel indignant by saying how dare you for thinking that they did something wrong by forgetting their promise. They might even blame you and your "high standards" for the fact that they failed to realize their promise.

Narcissistic spouses will only do something if they know they can get something out of it. They won't mow the lawn, wash the dishes, or run errands for you if they know that these things will not be appreciated or rewarded. They always want to be credited for everything that they do. If it goes unnoticed, prepare to listen to their ranting about it.

Humility is definitely out of reach. As mentioned before, their first priority will always be themselves.

They are not even ashamed of being selfish and feeling entitled.

They do not recognize boundaries. Narcissists are used to crossing personal boundaries if it means getting to their goal. It could be to hurt you or another person and they won't apologize for it.

Narcissists are not capable of loving and caring. They do have feelings, but these are all based on certain conditions. Usually, they will show the motions of loving you if they know that you can boost their ego by supporting their grandiose view of themselves. If you disagree with them, then don't expect them to show their fake love and warmth.

How to end a fight with a narcissist

Fighting with a narcissist is more than just engaging a regular opponent. Narcissists are fueled by their fear and paranoia, especially when they tend to assume that other people think and behave the same way that they do. They would think that other people also ridicule and judge them, abandon them, and cheat on them, because these are the things that they actually do.

The worst thing about this is that all these fears are based solely on their imagination. Their disorder makes them behave this way. In many cases, this behavior is not based on the behavior of their past or current partners. They are convinced that other people would treat them the way they treat others.

The truth is no one wants to follow in their footsteps because of how rotten their behavior and personality is. They might even be losing friends and family in the process as narcissism eats them up over time.

Still, it is hard to fight with them or to even try to talk sense into them because they have already led themselves to believe in something beyond reality. If you have unintentionally started a fight with them, it might be better for you to disengage now. Leave them alone to reflect on some things in their life. This might help them realize that they are the cause of their own failure in life.

How to love a narcissist

Do you think you will ever be ready to deal with a narcissist, let alone love one? You can't do anything much about having narcissistic parents or siblings, and you may not have that much control to resist your love for a future spouse or partner.

Narcissists are actually easy to love. They are charming, successful, beautiful, and charismatic.

They know how to use compliments to draw people in, show their apparent interest in you, and set the trap with their exciting and intellectual conversations. But beware, once you're in their trap, you have to deal with their selfishness, criticisms, demands, and offhand remarks. Your relationship will be all about them and their needs and it is up to you to cater to those needs.

At the start of a relationship, you might be basking under the confident aura of a narcissist. But it won't be long before you have to contend with their unpredictable moods, attacks, imaginary slights, and indignation. It is at this point in the relationship when you might start having doubts about your love for that person. If the narcissist is getting worse, you might even decide to get out of that relationship right away.

Eventually, you will lose yourself and your confidence in the middle of the relationship. The narcissist will ruin that for you by constantly pointing out your shortcomings and not forgetting about it at the dinner table either. Many narcissists are perfectionists, possibly due to the thought that they can do no wrong themselves. That's why they don't know how to appreciate your efforts or acknowledge them. If you confront them about it, you might have to deal with their rage and hurt. They are highly sensitive people, especially when you are giving them criticisms.

Narcissists do not see you as an individual with a life of your own. Instead, you are simply someone who exists to cater to their whims. They might not even pay attention to your condition as long as they are set out to get what they need from you. They expect to be entitled to constant love, care, praise, and service. They also expect for you to know how to please them. Another thing that you ought to remember about them is that they don't react well to a "no." They are used to getting a "yes." They would even react negatively when you try to set boundaries. Narcissists have also mastered the art of manipulating people, in a way that you will feel absolutely guilty for denying them of their request. They can make you feel useless and not worth their attention if you start going against them. Prepare to accept all the blame and punishments and the lack of love, care, and attention once you start to say no to them.

Compassion is the key towards learning how to love a narcissist. Just think about how they didn't choose their disorder and the way they behave. As you learn to see beyond their negative behavior, you will see their vulnerability deep inside.

Avoid exposing them

Exposing the narcissist and getting the "truth" out for all to see can be appealing and feels like the right thing to do. You may think this is the best solution for them, you and anyone else involved - that they will suddenly see clearly and take responsibility for changing their behavior. Forget about being right for a moment and bringing the truth to light.

Pointing out that the narcissist is not as wonderful as think they are can result in a huge backlash, that you then must be around, and may not be able to escape. They are not ever going to agree with you, as they are tied to their elevated identity. Rather than changing their minds, they will be more likely to simply despise you for your opinions.

Narcissists can also be extremely vindictive. If you burst their bubble, they will regroup, and may well come back to make you pay. They may "rally the troops" and loyal fans that they have and turn others against you through whatever means they see as necessary. If the narcissist is in a position of power over you, this can be an especially dangerous place to be.

Admire and listen to them

Being amenable is probably the most passive technique that you can take. As long as you are not already on the narcissist's "naughty list," it can be really effective at pulling you through difficult times until you reach calmer waters or are able to end the relationship. Clinical psychologist Al Bernstein suggests that remaining quiet and allowing the narcissist to come up with reasons to congratulate themselves is easy, effortless and requires nothing more than listening and looking interested.

Admiring them, their achievements, and qualities as much as they do can be a fast route into their "good books." So long as you avoid getting too close, this position in their good books can allow you to maintain a happier status quo with the narcissist still in your life.

Don't reject them

Rejecting a narcissist, whether in reality or in their perception, is likely to make them feel incredibly hurt or angry - as it causes a deep narcissistic injury. A jilted lover may feel a great deal of pain when the source of their affection no longer wants them. So too a narcissist feels deeply aggrieved when a source of narcissistic supply - or anyone else for that matter - decides that they are not "good enough."

Being too busy or not having a good enough reason to deny their request for your company or collaboration can easily be taken to heart, and result in an unexpectedly intense response. It's best to give them a legitimate reason that is beyond your control than to show that you're choosing to reject them. Being too busy to meet or see them is best if your reason is irrefutable, like having to work late to meet a specific deadline, attend an important wedding, or you are booked onto a vacation or trip elsewhere.

Avoid showing weaknesses or needs, and give them an "out" when they attack

If you show a narcissist what it is that makes you vulnerable, or what it is that you really want, they may at some point use it against you when they want to manipulate you. Narcissists will frequently learn what it is that you want most from them and set about denying it so that you are in a constant state of "need." If a narcissistic mother does this, she may control her children through their neediness for her love. The same goes for a romantic partner. They'll ration your supply of what you enjoy most from them to keep you controllable and pliable.

If they know your greatest concerns or fears they may leverage these to manipulate you. They may even use you as a distraction from their own inner turmoil when they are experiencing crashing self-esteem, by needling you on your points of weakness, to make themselves feel strong again.

You can give them the opportunity to stop playing manipulative games by offering them an "out" such as: "You're being uncharacteristically pessimistic today. You're usually such an optimist. Is there anything wrong?" In doing so, you call them to return to their "higher state of glory" without continuing their attack. Subconsciously they may even be aware that you successfully navigated their manipulation and decide to give you a wider berth in the future, or that they need to keep you on their side.

If the attack is particularly vicious or nasty, avoiding emotions but maintaining a cool, calm and empathetic approach can work well to bring them back around. Whether you believe it or not, providing them with an excuse that effectively excuses their behavior will be much appreciated - as it helps them to avoid a crushing sense of shame and subsequent denial loops, and simply feel that they are understood and forgiven. You may even be surprised to find that this approach results in a voluntary concession and what may seem like the beginnings or a more responsible approach, but this is not something that should be anticipated or expected.

How to stop someone being a narcissist

Essentially, if someone is being unhealthily narcissistic, it is up to them to notice and correct their behavior, rather than anyone else to point it out to them and risk the backlash from a narcissistic injury. Healthy narcissism may work well, but it is important that it does not develop into a dependence on approval and attention to an extreme degree in the long-run.

Happily, we believe that narcissists are able to change the ways in which they see the world, but that this rarely happens. This is because, in the case of narcissists, many will live perpetually unaware or in denial of their skewed lens, and will never attempt to improve it.

To overcome narcissism, a first step is to recognize the role of addiction to narcissistic supply and stop attempting to secure it. Accepting that being ordinary is okay is essential, and that no matter what successes or failures life brings,a person can never become more than just a personequal to everyone else. The urge to stand out from the crowd needs to be quashed.

If it's impossible to stop supplying the ego, then aligning this need with a positive cause can at least make a difference in the world. Like any addiction, fighting it can be extremely difficult, and overcoming it whilst still being intoxicated is highly unlikely to happen. Rather than fighting to remain in control of narcissism, the narcissist must take responsibility for starving it and going "cold turkey," as with any alcoholic or drug addict.

Chapter 5:
Give them proof

Verify Any and All Claims That the Narcissist Makes

N arcissists are natural experts at lying. That is because they have learned to rationalize their lying, and they no longer feel any guilt the way ordinary people do when they mislead others. The next time the narcissist makes an outrageous claim, especially if it's about a mutual friend, take time to investigate the claim. Trust your own judgment about the person that the narcissist is making accusations against.

The most hardened narcissists could even pass polygraph tests while telling blatant lies because they are so adept at lying, that there is no cognitive dissonance that could cause a spike in their vitals. Some psychologists have come up with the hypothesis that narcissists lie about 80 to 90 percent of the time, and they even lie about petty and inconsequential things. Narcissists will only tell the truth when it benefits them.

To be safe, you have to treat every story you hear

97

from the narcissist with a lot of skepticism. You have to start with the assumption that everything is a lie until you prove otherwise. As you do your reality check, here are some things that you need to pay attention to in order to figure out what the actual facts are and what the narcissist is lying about:

If the narcissist casts him/herself as some kind of hero in the story, you can rest assured that you are being lied to. We have already discussed how the narcissist has an overinflated ego, so as he/she creates a fictional story to manipulate you, he/she won't be able to resist the urge to be the hero in the story. If a narcissist tells you that a friend of yours was talking ill about you, he/she will claim to have been your only advocate in that conversation.

In an attempt to seem heroic and superior, the narcissist will also come up with stories about meeting (or being friends) with famous people, going to exotic places, or being an instrumental part of some groundbreaking accomplishment that you may be vaguely familiar with. These stories are often unprompted or out of topic, but the narcissist will bend over backwards to make them seem relevant to the conversation that you are having.

As they try to manipulate you, one thing many narcissists tend to do is try to make themselves your best friend.So if the narcissist accuses a friend you have known for years of things that are clearly out of character, you should know that not only is he/she lying to you, it's likely that he/she is also telling similar lies about you to your friend in order to drive a wedge between the two of you.

In many cases, narcissists will also spin stories to cast themselves as victims, even though they are the actual perpetrators. When a narcissist gets in trouble with a third party, he/she will come to you telling stories about being wronged, being treated unfairly, and how he/she went out of the way to be the bigger person. Even if you were there and you witnessed the whole thing, you will find the narcissist trying to convince you that things didn't go down as you thought and that you were the one who didn't pay enough attention.

If you catch a narcissist doing something wrong, he/she may also try to get out of the situation by spinning a story about how he/she was messed up as a child or in a past relationship and that his/her bad behavior is a consequence of past traumatic events. The narcissist may try to get you to empathize with him/her by saying how he/she has been working on this one weakness and how you shouldn't give up on him/her. This kind of lie often works in a relationship in which you already feel invested. That kind of "confession" can make anyone seem endearing.

If a narcissist tells you that he is coming from a dark place, he is sorry, and he is on a journey to change his life, you should be greatly alarmed. If you let the narcissist off the hook because of a story like that, he is going to use the same story over and over again, and the more times you let it go, the harder it would be for you to take a different stance in the future.

When narcissists spin a story, they are going to inject a few half-truths into that story to make it seem more credible to you. You should be keen to note if the narcissist adds "facts" into the story, including places you are familiar with, days you vaguely recall, or people you used to know. The intention is to make you more inclined to believe him/her. You should pay attention to the unnecessary details that the narcissist throws into the story, and the detail he/she brings to your attention with a bit of emphasis. Then, if you can, fact-check those details. More often than not, they are all lies.

It Is Okay to Say No

It is easy for us to fall back into our old ways and to even allow the narcissist back into our lives. This is especially difficult not to do because of the attachment and love we feel towards them. But when they initiate a conversation, we must remember our boundaries. We must remember how hard we are working in order to heal. We can listen to their sob story but we must not allow them back in. Remember why you are trying to heal. Experiencing what you did again will be detrimental to your mental health. We must remove our own emotions from the new way of thinking in which we are currently trying our best to see through to the end.

We have to understand that a narcissist operates in the singular with such fanaticism that they do not care about what we are feeling. The only reason they want you back in their life is because they know you are vulnerable and they want to exploit this. This is a common factor with narcissistic mothers and their daughters.

However, in terms of the much broader narcissist spectrum, we must learn to say "no". Saying no is quite possibly the most important tool in the human vocabulary. No means no and should remain so. Do not take the advances of the narcissist with that attachment. Detachment from that relationship is why you are healing and to do otherwise would jeopardize all that you have accomplished so far in your healing process.

It is hard to say no, but once we learn to say no, we can successfully build on our new emotional foundations to find that growth that comes from healing. It is important to be who you want to be and to continue your journey of self-discovery in order to heal.

Chapter 6:
Make a promise

The most important thing you need to do now so you don't remain stuck in indecision.

You have to get away from the narcissist because staying is not good for you in the long-run. However, there are situations where the narcissist in question is a vital part of your life, and it's utterly impractical for you to leave him/her completely. For instance, he/she could be a spouse with whom you have kids, a family member, or a colleague in your department. In such cases, you can try to put as much distance between the two of you as possible, while at the same time trying to limit the harm that befalls your kids, your other family members or your career respectively.

If your lives aren't already intertwined, you can break up with them, leave them, and avoid contacting them altogether. Remember that they didn't really care about you, so don't worry too much about how they are going to feel after you break up.

Don't bother explaining in too much detail why you are leaving. Remember that if you take the time to

103

justify yourself, they are going to try to talk you out of it. Break up in a public place and leave, never to return. Don't agree to be friends with them or to hang out in the future, no matter how insistent they are.

Some psychologists even suggest that you should break up with narcissists over the phone because there is no way of telling how in-person meetings are going to go. When you avoid contact with the narcissist, tell him that he is not welcome into your home, and block his number from your phone. If you leave the tiniest window open, he is going to find a way to crawl back into your life. Don't do any lingering goodbye. Just say your peace and leave.

There are always going to be some mutual friends who are going to vouch for the narcissist and tell you that you made a mistake leaving him. These friends may mean well, but they certainly don't fully understand how much you have been suffering under the thumb of the narcissist. With them, you have to make it clear that the narcissist is persona non grata, and the cost of bringing him up during your conversations is that they will lose your friendship. Tell them that you don't want any updates on the narcissist's life, and if they still talk to him, they shouldn't tell him anything about you either.

When you leave a narcissist, that very same day, write down exactly why you left him. In your journal, put down the rationale for your decision, and all the reasons why being with him was a bad thing for you. The purpose of this is that when the narcissist comes crawling back into your life and tries to manipulate you, you can refer back to your journal and remember why it's vital that you stay away from him. We have talked about gas lighting and how a manipulative narcissist can get you to question your own sanity, so having contemporaneous records of your thoughts and feelings can help you stay grounded in the truth.

If you successfully get away from a narcissist, hopefully, he/she will move on quickly, find someone else to torment, and leave you alone. Because the narcissist never really cared about you in the first place, he won't be too hung up on your relationship, so don't question your decision when you see that he/she has moved on too quickly and you start to worry that you may end up alone. Being alone is better than being with someone who sucks the life out of you.

Ignore the Narcissist

The narcissist lives to trigger emotional reactions in people because, in their minds, that gives them some sense of power. If a narcissist causes you to lose control over your emotions, it gives him a lot of satisfaction. When a narcissist attacks you verbally, ignoring him can drive him crazy.

You have to understand that narcissists crave attention, so ignoring them hurts them more than anything else. They want to be acknowledged and validated; that is why they start with the conflict in the first place. When a narcissist targets you and destroys your life, your natural instinct will be to get back at him/her by reacting angrily and emotionally, but if you do that, you are only playing into his/her hand.

It may not seem so at first, but over time, you will realize that ignoring the narcissist is actually much more satisfying than engaging with him/her because then, even to third-party observers, the narcissist will just seem like a petty person who likes to pick fights with people, and you will seem like the mature adult who is able to rise above it all.

The narcissist wants to control you and to assert dominance over you, but you have to remember that people can't take power from you. You actually have to give it to them. A narcissist can only have dominance over you if you relinquish control to him/her. As we have mentioned, you are guaranteed to lose if you play the narcissist's game, and that is when he/she is actually capable of dominating you. By ignoring the narcissist, you blatantly refuse to play his/her game, and then he/she has no means with which to get close enough to have any form of control over your life.

In as much as ignoring the narcissist hurts him/her, remember that you are doing it for yourself and for your own peace of mind. When you choose to ignore a narcissist, don't be preoccupied with the effect that the lack of attention has on him/her. Focus on doing something worthwhile for yourself. If after ignoring the narcissist, you are still obsessed with how he/she is reacting to it, then you are still under his/her control, and you are relinquishing your power to him/her. When you ignore an ex who is a narcissist, don't turn around and start stalking him on social media to see if he is miserable. Now that you have regained control, you should focus on detoxifying from the narcissist's influence and training yourself to be more vigilant in the future. If the narcissist is someone who is in your life permanently, ignoring him/her is going to be a regular thing, so you have to train yourself so as to get better at it. Ignoring a narcissist is more than just avoiding responding to their taunts. It's about learning to stop caring about their opinions and their criticisms. The first step is to restrain yourself from responding to them even if their comments hurt you, but after that, you have to work on yourself to get to the point where what they say rolls off you like water.

When you ignore a narcissist, you have to keep your safety in mind. Some narcissists tend to turn aggressive or violent when you deny them attention, so you have to be careful not to be anywhere with them without witnesses present. Ignoring a narcissist makes him/her feel that you have slipped away from his/her control, and in a desperate effort to regain that control, you never know how they are going to lash out. You have to be a lot more cautious and a lot smarter going forward because the narcissist is going to bring his/her "A" game in order to regain control over you. Keep ignoring them, and no matter how hard they come at you, don't relent, not even slightly.

Why up to 74% of marriages are failing right now and what to do about it for your own life so you're not just another statistic.

Wouldn't it be a wonderful world if everyone was honest and had some written message on their person making clear their intentions and motivations... Unfortunately, this is not the case. Yet, in terms of marriage and partnership, the games and deceptions of a narcissist do not make for the best partner. In fact, there is no partnership present at all; perhaps only in fleeting moments. Partnership implies unity, harmony, and a mutual respect, trust and connection. All a narcissist has to offer is mind games, suffering, confusion and oppression. It can be highly oppressive living and being with a narcissist as they don't like to see you happy, thriving or succeeding in your own personal goals, dreams and aspirations.

Narcissists are extremely controlling. They see their partner as a target or supply for their deep-seated manipulations and need to control. Fortunately, you can spot this tendency early on, creating better boundaries and inner strength. It can be more difficult once you are already enticed and wrapped around their little finger, but if you can remain strong and centered from the start then there shouldn't be a problem with recognizing this sign that you are with a narcissist.

This control reflects into many areas. It may be the clothes you wear, your beliefs, your daily habits and actions, your likes and dislikes, and your holistic identity and sense of self. Whichever the expression, you are simply not allowed to be you or be free to make your own life choices.

You will know you are with a narcissist when their

deeply buried insecurities start to come to light. They will always be masked as arrogance, a false sense of superiority, self-centeredness, an inflated ego, and other less desirable personality traits. Real displays of vulnerability, raw emotion, and low feelings or moods which are natural and a part of our humanity will never be shown. Wounds, traumas, doubts, fears, and general self-discovery or self-development are all covered by a need to appear the best, all together, omniscient and forcefully superior. There is no sense of room and space for healing and in the narcissist's eye they are already perfect. They want you to believe they are perfect too, and anything which threatens their sense of self-created status is met with abuse, manipulation or projection-like tactics.

In marriage, the narcissist receives your love and support which further empowers them and keeps their narcissistic ways in a sense of acceptance. If there is no support, then there is no acceptance. Something cannot exist without the energy, awareness and thumbs up from people. It is we human beings who create and shape reality as we know it. This is one of the key reasons why a narcissist gets married, because they know that their illusions will only survive and thrive through the support of another. Again, you become like their rock or gem. This support may be unconscious or based on you being fooled and stuck in their games, however it is still a green light.

However, to the narcissist marriage is a means of escape. They can escape from their past, their wounds, their narcissism and their often 'evil' and sadistic intentions; through the presence and cover of a life partner. They are incapable of having a healthy, intimate and cooperative or supportive relationship and the lack of empathy and compassion is too prevalent to overlook. Even if you are strong beyond belief, you will still be the sufferer in the marriage due to the narcissist's ability to break your heart over and over.

Why it's CRITICAL you choose wisely with whom you discuss your struggling marriage and why the wrong choice can end a marriage worth saving.

Go to your support system and people you trust. Ask their opinion about the person you think might be a narcissist. In many cases, when you are getting close to someone, it can be difficult to see their flaws. However, your close friends and family are on the outside looking in and can pick up on issues faster and easier than you can. Just remember that if their opinions are negative, do not get defensive. They care about you and want to ensure that you are surrounded by good people. The importance of peer, family and friendship support cannot be disregarded when divorcing a narcissist. Your ability to manage conflict is largely tied in with the amount of support you receive. It can be both a coping mechanism and essential aspect to your recovery and conflict resolution. Narcissists thrive off the social support and cooperation of others.

As in all great endeavors, a support network is crucial. These are people you can fall back on for advice, support, or even just a quiet ear to listen in tough times. As NPD becomes more recognized and more people find themselves surrounded by narcissists, support groups have become more common. A quick web search of "narcissistic abuse survivor support" will yield a wealth of resources, both in person and online.

Being able to speak to other people who truly understand your struggles, your journey, and what you have gone through is incredibly validating. You feel understood and legitimized and you find other people who have been in your shoes who may be further down the route to healing than you are. These are people who will not try to pick apart your experiences or try to sidestep the issues you are dealing with. They understand what it means to be vulnerable to a narcissist and having them on your side will provide clearer insight for you.

Seeing people who are further in their healing journey than you also has the added benefit of showing you that there is hope and there is a life after the narcissist has been removed from your life. You begin to see what life can be, and that can be one of the most valuable assets to you when you find yourself feeling vulnerable or weak. Remembering that the person from your support group said it does get harder before it gets easier can give you the little push you need in order to continue moving forward. The motivation and encouragement from people who were in your shoes not too long ago can be invaluable when you feel like you cannot keep climbing an endless mountain. These people show you that the mountain does, in fact, have a summit, even if you cannot see it yet, and the only way you will ever reach the summit is if you keep moving forward.

Through the internet, you may also find support groups specific to the narcissistic relationship you found yourself in. With a few specific web searches, you can locate an online community for narcissistic romantic partners, friends, parents, siblings, relatives, co-parents or any other type of narcissist you may have in your life. Despite the fact that you may have a rare type of narcissist in your life, the internet connects us all, and you will be able to find others who have similar experiences to you, who can give advice tailored to your specific situation instead of general advice to handling narcissists.

Chapter 7:
Create a sense of urgency

If you can't stay, then Get away from them

Sometimes, despite your best efforts, a relationship becomes toxic and unbearable. No matter how hard you try or what you do, the narcissist continuously hurts you emotionally, and you are feeling less and less like yourself. In these cases, it is time to draw a line in the sand and walk away. Walking away is not the easy way out, despite what those around you might say; it will require immense self-discipline and willpower to walk away from someone you may deeply love, and it is okay to do so when you are being hurt.

Abuse is always a reason to end a relationship, even if it is caused by a mental illness or disorder. While you may have sworn in sickness and in health in wedding vows, that did not include a risk to your own health. You must take care of yourself before you are able to help anyone else, and if you feel as if you are being abused or mistreated, leaving is totally acceptable. Think of this as the ultimate boundary: You do not expect to on the receiving end of intentional harm, physical or emotional, from the other person. When that person intentionally harms you, that line has been irrevocably crossed, and the thought of the other person doing that again will always loom in the background, coloring your relationship. You do not have to live like that. You are entitled to live a life free of pain, and with the respect every person deserves.

Even when a relationship does not involve physically harming you, sometimes the emotional toll it takes is too much. You find yourself constantly drained and like you can no longer enjoy the things that used to bring you pleasure. People may be telling you that you seem depressed, but in reality, you are drained by a relationship. Perhaps your parent is always downplaying every achievement you have, to the point that you believe that you are worthless and incapable of success. Maybe your best friend is constantly one-upping you, so you feel like you are wrong to feel proud of whatever accomplishments you achieve because she is always better. It could be a coworker who belittles and berates you every time you make a mistake, no matter how small.

Regardless of what the nature of the relationship is, taking a step back and cutting the narcissist off is almost always an option. When an entire cut-off is not possible due to sharing minor children, or because you live in such close proximity to the other person, you can take a huge step back and keep the relationship and interactions with the person as minimal as possible to avoid further exposure to their toxicity. It may not be easy, but just as you would not willingly spend time around a rattlesnake just because you have plenty of antivenom readily available, you should not spend time around toxic people. Their toxicity will eat away at you as time goes by, rendering you a husk of your former self.

After cutting off or limiting contact with the narcissist, you will begin to feel more like your old self, and you may realize just how much of a toll that relationship had taken. In hindsight, you may suddenly see all of the red flags and wonder how you managed to get yourself ensnared in such a big mess in the first place. Remember, narcissists are typically masters at manipulating people around them, feeling it is necessary to their survival and mental health to do so. You are not the first, and you will not be the last person to get ensnared in a toxic narcissist's web of lies, and you should not beat yourself up over it after deciding to break free.

Typically, extreme narcissists lack normal levels of empathy, don't pull their own weight, and tend to make the people close to them miserable within the space of a few weeks or months. They are unlikely to have a great deal of insight into their damaging behaviors and are unlikely to have an epiphany compelling them to change.

Although it may be a very difficult consideration, none of us must remain in contact with anybody if the other party is causing us serious emotional damage. But taking the drastic step of cutting them off permanently could well be something that will live with us for many years to come and should not be taken lightly.

Less drastic steps include taking a break or managing the situation. Breaks can help to gain clarity, but it depends upon the relationship at hand, and whether you deem it to be worth saving. It's important to choose the people you spend time with wisely, because humans tend to adopt the characteristics of those around them.

A person leaving a narcissistic relationship will probably go back a few times before finally breaking contact. A narcissist is unlikely to just 'let it go'. As we've mentioned previously in this book, many narcissists want to have the best of the best, and they collect things as possessions. In some ways, their partner is an extension of that. When their partner chooses to leave them, they see this as a failure and a huge rejection. They will react either with anger, or they will attempt to charm them back, reverting to the 'old' version which initially attracted the person to them in the first place. In many cases, this can be enough to get their partner to return to them because they still have deep feelings underneath it all.

Many partners who leave this type of relationship require a large amount of support afterwards, and some even require emotional counseling. Depending upon the type of treatment they have been subjected to (far worse in the event of being close to a toxic or malignant narcissist), the empath may find it extremely difficult to have trusting and healthy relationships in the future, without some kind of therapy or support.

As you can see, narcissistic relationships aren't just damaging for the narcissist (because many end up missing out on genuine loving unions as a result of their inability to have healthy relationships), but also for the partner too. Leaving it difficult, and in some cases, it can be a process which takes months, if not years.

It's often the case that they know their partner is narcissistic towards the end. This is usually the catalyst for making them think they should leave.

However, when gas lighting begins, the difficulty really turns itself up a notch or two.

Though narcissistic abuse doesn't usually involve violence or physical harm to the victim, that's not a guarantee – especially when your abuser finds out you intend to leave. There may also be few limits to what your abuser is capable of doing to make you stay, from taking away your means of doing so to convincing you that you've made a mistake.

Even if you are already free, there are certain steps you may not have taken that it would be a good idea to still do, if you feel that your abuser has not yet accepted the split.

1. Make sure you have all of your important personal documents stored in a safe place away from your abuser. Take copies of all of them and ask a trusted friend or family member to keep hold of them for you.

2. Change the passwords on all of your online accounts, especially email, bank accounts and social media.

3. Arrange a place to stay with someone you trust or with a hotel that you can easily get to. Make sure to confirm with the hotel owner or your friend that they must not let your abuser know where you are.

4. In the days before you leave, try to refrain from telling too many people your plans – or even that you are going to leave. Especially for people who know both of you, you could be placing them in a difficult position and there is no guarantee they won't feel obliged to share what they know with your abuser.

Once you have left, avoid all contact with your abuser. If you feel compelled to offer an explanation, do so in a letter beforehand. Your abuser is likely to demand that you "owe" them an explanation or a second chance. You are vulnerable at this moment – it can take every ounce of a person's emotional capability to be as brave as you were when you closed that door behind you. Even had your abuser not taken advantage of your good nature already, at this moment you must put yourself first and take care of your needs. Listening to their manipulation is nowhere on that list of needs.

Resist the temptation to engage your abuser again from this new place of strength. Yes, you are now better equipped to deal with them. Yes, you are now able to see the traps before you step in them. But no, they will not ever change and they cannot ever be a positive part of your life, in any capacity. And there will be no closure, because a narcissist is not able to see their behavior for what it is – they lack empathy and the emotional depth to do so.

Let go of your abuser forever; shed all contact if possible or keep it limited if not. Keep your emotions in check if you have no choice but to see them – remember they will be using any weapons at their disposal to bring you back in line and all of these weapons play with your emotions. Take a step back from yourself and look at the situation as though you were gazing on one of your diary entries. If it helps, remember that there is nothing so frustrating to a narcissist as not being able to elicit a reaction from you.

Understand What Is Required if you decide to stay in the relationship

If you decide to establish and/or maintain a relationship with a narcissist you should know that there will be a lot required of you. A huge amount of your time will be needed and your presence will be demanded.

Yes, narcissists can express their love for you but they will also require you to reciprocate that love or to at least express it profoundly in return. You see, you will have to assure narcissists in order to appease their anxieties.

There will be times when it will be like you need to give unconditional love. Well, sometimes that is exactly what a narcissist will want from you.

Some narcissists fear abandonment and they will do everything—and I do mean everything—to keep you with them. Well, that is if they have grown to love you. But remember that there will be many days when it will be like they are pushing you away.

They will be angry at you, they will put you down, and even insult you. Sometimes it will feel like the narcissist is pushing you away. But then again you'll be dragged back into loving arms.

Remember that they will be driven by this seemingly illogical need for approval. Because of that they will do things that will seem to sabotage your relationship. It's a cycle really—a crazy cycle of love and hate.

Nevertheless, there is no harm in trying to love a narcissist even if the one you're trying to love has severe symptoms of NPD. There will be people who will not understand why you're putting up with all the bad treatment.

Some would even say that your narcissist doesn't deserve you. And that is part of the package—there will be pressure within the relationship and there will be pressure from without.

123

Just remember that the bottom line here is that you chose to be in this relationship, not them. It's a gamble and you can't play it without being fully into it.

When you find yourself unable or unwilling to cut off a narcissist, there are other ways to protect yourself from the narcissist's manipulation and harmful behaviors. One of those ways is setting healthy boundaries. Healthy boundaries are necessary to protect yourself when interacting with other people. They represent the line that others know not to cross when dealing with you and create a divide between yourself and others. Boundaries are healthy for everyone, including married couples or parents and children. It is important to note that you can have a relationship where you tell each other everything but still have boundaries; the boundaries are behaviors you refuse to tolerate, not walls that you set up to push other people away. A healthy boundary may be expecting to be treated with a certain level of respect or insisting that you will not tolerate name-calling or other demeaning behavior. Most people would agree that not being called names is an acceptable boundary and will not cross it.

Maintaining Yourself

When dealing with a narcissist, you find yourself

having to make plenty of concessions to avoid meltdowns or outrages. With narcissists, you often feel as if you have to make a choice between pleasing yourself or the narcissist, and it's frequently easier to forego what you want than it is to deal with the backlash from the narcissist. It is important to make sure you maintain your own sense of self during the process of dealing with a narcissist, and you need to be able to understand what the appropriate steps are to maintaining yourself. You need to know when flexibility is useful or if setting boundaries will be a better course of action. You also need to understand when enough is enough so you can take a step back from the situation and disengage from the narcissist for your own physical and emotional safety. Learning these skills will give you a much better grasp of how to interact with a narcissist while minimizing damage for everyone involved.

Bending, Not Breaking

Just as the tree bends to the wind to keep from breaking, sometimes being flexible with your own expectations is the best choice when it comes to dealing with a narcissist. Narcissists are stubborn by nature; they want everything to go their way and struggle to cope when things do not play out as they expect. The average person is much better at coping with small missteps in their plans without being

125

tripped up, and sometimes, the easiest way to maintain yourself and your sanity is to remain flexible. If the concession is something you truly do not care about, it is likely not worth the battle of remaining firm. Pick your battles and let the narcissist have her way if you are indifferent.

Your own self-awareness and self-restraint will be two of your greatest defenses against falling victim to narcissistic behaviors. Unlike the narcissist, you can recognize when you are wrong without sending your world shattering around you, and you can also restrain yourself when something does go wrong. You have developed proper coping mechanisms and have learned to handle stress in healthy, productive ways that do not worsen your problems. Remembering to utilize your self-awareness will keep you aware that you are angry or frustrated with the narcissist. This recognition allows you to be aware that you may be more prone to lashing out at the narcissist at that moment, which also allows you to utilize your self-restraint. You can remind yourself to stop, take a deep breath, and count to four before reacting to keep from impulsively lashing out.

Remember, by remaining flexible when applicable, you keep yourself from breaking. Your flexibility keeps you strong and able to withstand the difficult behaviors that come from the narcissist. Your patience will keep you firm as you encounter the same issues over and over, and your self-awareness will help you acknowledge your feelings so you can cope with them in a healthy, productive way.

Specific tips to give your marriage any hope of feeling good again that you can implement in your marriage starting today.

Narcissists are notorious for inflicting pain to everyone around them. While it may not always be intentional, the results are undeniable. People end up hurt and broken when in the narcissist's inner circle. It is difficult to manage dealing with a narcissist and coming out of the interactions relatively unscathed, but with the right skill set, you will be able to minimize the injuries inflicted by the narcissist's scathing personality. Remember, not all of these methods will work for every narcissist. Through trial and error, you will be able to discover the best way to handle the particular narcissist in your life. The end results will be worth the immense amount of effort it will take to remove the narcissist's target from your back, as you will find your life much more peaceful once you begin to implement these methods of coping with a narcissist.

Take a Time-out

When tensions run high, and you find yourself creeping closer and closer to your breaking point, it is entirely acceptable to take a time out from your relationship with a narcissist. During this period, you completely ignore all contact from the narcissist and put distance between you and him. The goal here is to give yourself the space you need in order to begin healing from the narcissist's toxicity. By giving yourself time to cool off, you keep yourself from exploding or making the situation exponentially worse by saying something you do not mean in your anger. The time out can have a specific time limit, such as asking for a week of space or can be indefinite with you waiting until you no longer feel like screaming every time you see the narcissist. The important thing here is to set the time limit to what you need, rather than catering to anyone else or compromising on the length.

Cut off the narcissist

Similar to taking a time-out, cutting off the narcissist involves taking a step back from the situation altogether. However, unlike a time-out, cutting off is typically a permanent severance of the relationship. The only way to truly avoid any more harm, whether emotionally or physically, is to refuse to engage or associate with the narcissist completely. By never being near the narcissist or never acknowledging the narcissist, the narcissist never has the opportunity to hurt you.

Refusing to engage with the narcissist also comes with a secondary benefit: you have cut off the narcissist's strongest motivator. By refusing to be a source of the narcissistic supply he craves, the narcissist eventually loses interest in you and instead will move onto someone else who will provide him with his fix.

Disengage Emotionally

Recognize that NPD is a personality disorder; the narcissist literally has a disordered way of thinking, and therefore, the narcissist's perceptions about the world around him should not be used as a measure of the truth. Remember that the narcissist seeks to manipulate others to get what he wants and cannot see the world in a realistic manner. He will say things and believe things that are untrue just so it fits his own paradigms of the world around him. Just because his way of seeing the world is skewed and disordered does not mean you have to accept it.

By disengaging emotionally, you hear what he says and briefly acknowledge it, but do not take it seriously. Just as you would not care much when an angry child calls you a doo-doo head, you should not care much when the narcissist screams that you are a horribly selfish person that would be better off dead because at least then, more than one person would benefit from your life insurance or estate. While it can be hard to ignore what the narcissist says, especially if the narcissist is someone you have held in high regard in the past, such as a spouse or a parent, you must remember that it is not true. By refusing to become upset at the narcissist's accusations, you protect your self-esteem, and when you refuse to fall victim to the narcissist's tactics, the narcissist slowly loses interest in you as well.

Manage Expectations and Focus on Positives

When dealing with narcissists, it becomes exponentially easier when you recognize the limits of the narcissist's personality. Especially when you actively want to maintain a relationship with a narcissist, whether personal, romantic or professional. By understanding who the narcissist is and not expecting him to be someone he is not, you can eliminate a lot of heartbreak. Do not expect the narcissist ever to be a valid form of support for you, as he will never have the empathy necessary for that. The narcissist will not be a source of comfort for you, and if you can accept that and set up outside support systems, you can create a mindset that lets you enjoy the aspects of the narcissist you may enjoy. This does not mean you should simply accept their abusive tendencies; you should absolutely continue to correct any time the narcissist boundary stomps.

When interacting with the narcissist, it can be useful to remind yourself about the parts you enjoy. Perhaps the narcissist is a perfectionist by nature, so you know you can rely on him to create the perfect cake for a party. Not only does that feed the narcissist's ego in a healthy way, but it also reminds you of the good in the narcissist. Very few people are truly evil, and the good traits the narcissist possesses are important to embrace when maintaining a relationship. Maybe the narcissist is really good at a video game you enjoy, so you have fun playing with him, or perhaps the narcissist is a natural, albeit harsh, leader and you find that you can learn a lot in a professional setting. With your expectations managed and placing emphasis on the narcissist's redeeming features, you may find it easier to tolerate some of the more annoying, but harmless, narcissistic tendencies.

Studying them

You need to study the narcissist, not from the perspective of a loved one, but from that of an outsider. If you cannot do this, then none of the other tips discussed in this section will work. When you objectively start studying the narcissist, you will better be able to learn how to detach yourself mentally and emotionally. If you can analyze the behavior of a narcissist in a dispassionate manner, then it will give you the clarity you need to restore your emotional balance.

Call out

Most narcissists tend to be quite proud of their narcissism and think of it as a positive personality trait. You must call out the narcissist for their narcissistic ways. This will only work if the narcissist also values and cherishes the relationship you share. If that's the case, then use a measured and non-sarcastic tone to tell the narcissist that their narcissism is showing.

Feed their ego

A narcissist needs a lot of attention, affection, praise, and adoration to thrive. So, by complimenting him and feeding his fragile ego, you can easily handle living with a narcissist. You must be prepared to keep feeding his ego, if not, be prepared to deal with his tantrums. This is something you will need to get used to if leaving the narcissist is not an option for you. A couple of simple compliments can go a long way while trying to deal with a narcissist. This is not manipulation. Instead, it is about understanding his personality disorder and using it to help smooth things out.

Manage your expectations

Narcissists lack empathy. They certainly expect sympathy from others, but will seldom reciprocate. This absence of empathy makes it difficult for a narcissist to develop close and intimate bonds with others. You need to learn to accept and make peace with this. So, stop seeking empathy or compassion from the narcissist and instead try to manage your expectations.

Find Yourself

To find yourself again, you need to step back and view yourself from afar. This means evaluating your current state in detail and then looking at that evaluation from an objective distance.

The best way to do this is to remove your thoughts and emotions from your own mind and put them somewhere else, where you can examine them more clearly. A great way to do this is to begin a daily journal, pouring all your emotions and the thoughts you've had onto paper. Make sure to concentrate on how you feel, not just on the events that made you feel that way.

Other alternatives include painting or drawing or writing your feelings in the form of poetry. Choose a medium that you feel suits you and will allow you to take what's happening on your head and put it on paper instead. It can take practice, especially if you're not used to giving voice to your emotions, but it's very important that you put every last piece of you onto that paper.

Take time every day for this activity. Close yourself into a private space where you won't be interrupted and where nobody else can see what you are creating. This is just for you – keep the results somewhere secure, so you don't have to worry that anyone else will ever see them.

Creating a mirror of yourself in this way not only allows you to pour out all the damaging emotions in a safe way, it also allows you to see them outside yourself. It allows you to see the true you, and the progress you are making, and the progress you still need to make.

Rebalance Your Life

A more formal version of this rediscovery of who you are and what you want is to reintroduce balance into your life. This is about what you need as well as what you want and involves rebuilding a balance that may have been toppled by your abuser's actions.

Your abuser may have removed your connection to friends, they may have insisted you live and work in places that weren't really your choice, they may have chosen your hobbies for you by demanding you do the things they wanted to do. One or more areas of your life may currently be lacking equilibrium, and it's time to bring that back.

The areas you will need to look at include:

- Your career (or future career if you are still in school)
- Your relationships
- Your living situation
- Your hobbies and interests
- Your beliefs

First, you will need to look at each of these areas in turn and ask yourself how the abuse affected them. Did, for example, your abuser mock your spiritual beliefs and make you feel guilty for wanting to attend services? Did they choose the apartment you rented because it was more convenient to them or suited their tastes and make you feel obliged to agree?

Once you have determined what changed in these areas of your life thanks to the abuse, you can think about what you want instead – and then make those

135

changes happen. As you do, think about the boundaries you want to set.

Tell yourself what you will and won't accept from outside influence in the future. For instance, you might say you will never again allow someone to stop you from attending your horse riding classes because they are important to your happiness and your sense of self. Perhaps you will pledge to yourself that you will always attend Thanksgiving with your family and that there would need to be genuine negotiation before you broke that pledge.

How to protect yourself and your children from a narcissist

There are several ways to shield yourself and your kids from the narcissist in your life. The most important thing is for you to implement each one and stop that self-absorbed person.

You can convince yourself that you are actually safe in a narcissist's hands. However, their good person facade wouldn't last long, so you better brace yourself using a few strategies.

- Set boundaries. Know when you are at your limit in dealing with all the sarcastic remarks or hurtful things from a narcissist. At least you would know when to react after simply smiling and nodding to everything that a narcissist is saying or doing. By letting that person know your boundaries, he or she might at least be aware of it and possibly try to control their behavior.

- Determine the behaviors that are too much for you and tell them about these behaviors. While you're busy setting boundaries, you should not forget to tell the narcissist about excessive behaviors that you can no longer tolerate. List them and express why you don't like each one.

- Enjoy your down time more. Incorporate more rest into your daily schedule, especially a chance to get away from the narcissist for a breather. No matter how much you love that person, you might naturally feel suffocated too. Stay away from the negative vibes that a narcissist is emitting at home. Even the kids should be shielded from that person to avoid ruining their lives.

- Find a strong support group for yourself. While you might not be able to resist the need to whine and complain about your rotten, bad luck for being with a narcissist, support sessions should be spent more on renewing your energy and getting a fresh perspective on things. Take these times as your time to recharge and face the narcissist as a confident and self-assured individual after being ruined by their constant bullying and put-downs.

- Prepare a reserve. Aside from determining your boundaries, you should know when to strengthen them after years of being together with a narcissist. Take the time to repair the cracks in the foundation of your self-confidence.

- Stay strong and steady. Remain steadfast in your decision, whether to continue handling the narcissist, or staying away from the narcissistic relationship. Being neutral will also help.

- Be keen on spotting deceptions. Avoid being fooled into believing that you will still thrive with a narcissistic person. Tell your children about it too. Instead, try to look for real love, a love with no conditions and no self-centered behavior.

The real cause of the shift from wedded bliss to loneliness

Although being with a narcissist is a truly horrific

and often traumatic experience, breaking free can lead to initial loneliness. You are so used to being with that person, being involved in their stories, games, and sense of companionship even if it is a twisted and mentally-emotionally abusive companionship; that finally leaving and being free can leave you feeling empty. This is natural - we are all chalices waiting to be filled. We need connections, stories, relationships and various realities to keep us feeling alive and fulfilled. So when you break free from the narcissist you are essentially an empty vessel.

What new stories are you going to create?

This is of course, in itself, a beautiful process and fundamentally part of your journey. To be alone is to be all one, content, free and soulfully happy in your own independence. Once we remove attachments and stories which are no longer good for us, we provide ourselves the space and time for new stories, new realities and frequencies of being. I once heard the saying that life is like music. Life can be equated with music. We do live in a **uni**verse after all! So, loneliness can be overcome by filling yourself with new stories - ones in **harmony** with your best interests and best possible expression of you.

Connected to this is a self-recovery, healing and

boundary plan. Boundaries are very important, but so is your personal re-discovery of self and self-healing.

Below are the key and highly effective ways to overcome loneliness:

- Immerse yourself in a passion project. New hobbies, favorite pastimes or creating a vision board to align with your dreams and aspirations can all be marvelous gateways back to your true self. Following your greatest joy allows you to overcome loneliness and heal from the sufferings caused by your narcissistic partner. Passion and fire are the spark of life, they re-energize and revitalize your inner core further enabling you to stop feeling isolated or cut off from the world. This is an unfortunate consequence of being the victim of narcissistic abuse or mind manipulations - you may feel disconnected to others on a profound level. Re-finding yourself through a passion project is essential for your wellbeing.

- Recovering from a narcissist and re-finding yourself tie in closely to knowing yourself, or knowing thyself. Not only can taking steps to rediscover and know thyself help you overcome loneliness, it will also help increase your self-esteem, self-worth and personal confidence.

- Meditating can **reconnect** you to your true self, inner harmony, and a sense of peace and wellbeing. It also expands your mind and allows you to be an observer of any chaotic, destructive or afflictive thoughts, beliefs or emotions. During the many months or years of narcissistic abuse you will have been through some terrible manipulative treatment. You may have been gaslighted, made to feel small, weak or inferior, or generally insulted on repeat. Your feelings, opinions, and perspectives may have been overlooked and where your beautiful qualities and strengths should have been supported, encouraged and cherished; you instead received neglect and abuse. All in all, your partner knocked your confidence and self-esteem in many unseen ways.

Balanced with all the other key ways to overcome loneliness and heal for the long term is the engagement of new social groups and organizations. This can include peer support, groups for victims of narcissistic abuse, or simply any organization or venture which allows you to feel good. Being happy and connecting with others is the best way to let go and move forward with your life, despite the initial loneliness you may feel. You can feel lonely or isolated in a group too as the truth is - loneliness is just a mindset. Some people feel lonely even when surrounded by family and peers, just as many feel most at peace and blissful when alone. True happiness and contentment comes from your ability to connect and feel at ease with the world. Taking the first steps by putting yourself out there will re-spark your passion for life and connection, and your connection with yourself.

What to do when you have love for him...but aren't in love with him

People with narcissistic personality disorder always think of themselves and their needs first. Even if they might be able to carry a relationship with other people, that relationship tends to be more about them. Usually, the other person would feel ignored and devalued, damaging their self-esteem in the process. When that other person is you and you decide to break up with that self-centered person in your life, it can be dangerous, so you have to do it right.

The following steps have helped people break free from their narcissistic relationship:

- Go to therapy to assess the problem and your psychological condition. There are cases when the insurance might not cover it, or you cannot afford it, so an alternative would be to look for a support team. You can find it in domestic abuse shelters and women's advocate groups because you really are in an abusive relationship, even if it might not be a physical one. Learn everything about the right things to say and to do and determine the signs that you used to ignore about that other person being a narcissist.

- Use the feedback from your support group session to help you grieve as you deal with all the hurtful things that the narcissist is doing to you.

- If you are still together with the narcissist in your life and they know that you are trying to leave them, they might stop you from doing it. They might do it by embarrassing you, telling other people that you are "not good in the head," mess with your schedule, or anything else that will stop you from getting the support that you need. The more interruptions the narcissist does, the more you should try to seek help.

143

- Stop communicating with the narcissist. Some people often find themselves drawn into a relationship with the narcissist, as they are experts at making you feel good, at first. But that pleasant feeling isn't meant to last. They are good at laying down the trap. That is why you have to cut all contacts with that narcissist in your life. Some situations may even require moving to another place when the narcissist starts becoming violent. If you don't want to move, you can ask for help from your support group or the local law enforcement officials. You can even file for a restraining order to ensure your safety.

- Take self-defense classes. Enroll in a martial arts course or learn how to use a licensed weapon. Invest in a good guard dog for additional protection at home. Make it extra difficult for the narcissist to contact you, especially if you are also protecting children. The longer you can do this, the more confident you will be in your ability to shield yourself from the wrath of the abusive narcissist. Your confidence will further emphasize the fact that you are no longer the victim that you used to be.

- Write in a diary. Fill it with your thoughts every single day. Include the behaviors that the narcissist displays every day, especially those that triggered your doubts about their condition. Update your journal daily. This diary will help you in two significant ways – to strengthen your resolve to break free from that narcissistic relationship when you feel weak and to help you heal over time. Reading the words that you wrote yourself will help you realize how harmful your relationship has become with that person.

- Clean up your life of anything related to the narcissist. Get rid of all the things that will remind you of that person. Doing this is also about completely removing the influence that the person has in your life. Sell them, give them to charity, or throw them away.

- Establish new relationships, even if they are not necessarily romantic ones. Meeting new friends could be the best thing that could happen to you after breaking up with a narcissist. You can achieve that by getting involved in different organizations, such as a yoga class, book club, or pottery class. You don't even need to spend money. It's enough to get out of your home and find yourself some new friends. It helps you get back to your normal life without the narcissist in it.

- Allow yourself some time to grieve. It might be a good idea to enjoy your freedom from narcissism first before getting yourself involved in another relationship. The quicker you find yourself a rebound relationship, the riskier it might be to get attracted to another narcissist. You can grieve over a relationship that was based on an image that you saw wrongly of that person whom you used to love. Mourn your loss and the fact that you fell in love with an illusion. It is only natural that you will feel sad knowing that the person never loved you because he or she is incapable of loving anyone else other than themselves. This realization is enough reason to grieve. Use the time to get back to your normal self. Learn to love yourself more before you start loving another person again.

The ONE single thing you need to focus on at all times to find the clarity and confidence you Want - Self-Esteem

Self-esteem is all about being able to support yourself. It is about being able to take control of your mind, body, behavior and yourself in general. It is about your perception of yourself, the way you see yourself. It is about the influence you have on the environment around you. Do you think you have a positive effect on the world? Simply put, is the feedback you receive for your actions positive or negative? Do you feel like you don't have any effect whatsoever on the world around you? Do you feel that nothing seems to be going your way even when you are trying?

Well, self-destruction and sabotaging oneself are the opposite of self-esteem. You might notice that you indulge in doing things and thinking thoughts that sabotage your happiness, any success you attain, and the opportunities available to you. Self-destruction is when you don't talk well to yourself when you do things that are bad because of some self-hatred you are harboring within.

Developing your self-esteem can work wonders for you, especially while recovering from narcissistic abuse. Positive self-esteem makes you become more confident while facing life. It will not only make you happier, but it will also help you live better. The benefits of self-esteem are not restricted to just this. Your level of self-esteem is directly proportional to your level of confidence. Self-confidence is essential for self-respect and this, in turn, is proportional to the respect others give you. As people start to recognize you, the equation that you share with them improves, and all of this is bound to make you happier. On the other hand, low self-esteem often leads to depression, anxiety, low self-confidence, and dissatisfaction with yourself and everyone else around you. Low self-esteem will often make you question yourself, lessen your self-confidence, and prevent you from achieving anything you ever wanted. Most people do not like being with those who have low self-esteem because they also tend to dampen spirits of others as well.

In the same way that the emotions of others tend to affect you, your emotions also affect those around you. If all you project is negativity, it can be difficult to attract anything positive into your life. So, happy feelings give rise to more positive feelings whereas negativity merely attracts more negativity. People with positive self-esteem can see themselves in a positive light. They can love and respect themselves, and this helps them build positive relationships with others. Positive self-esteem gives confidence and the ability to work to achieve the goals you set for yourself. By working on developing your self-esteem, you can improve the quality of your life in general.

The best way for an emotional manipulator to gain

complete control over the victim is by lowering the victim's self-esteem. Once the victims start to feel like they are not worthy of anything good, they become putty in the hands of the manipulator. Those with low self-esteem tend to become lonely and avoid any personal relationship and interaction with others. It can even discourage one from believing in his dreams.

It is quite difficult to evaluate those who are near us, but this must be done. You should acknowledge those who bring nothing but negativity into your life and those who make a positive contribution to your life. Yes, it is a difficult task, but you must do it to avoid all individuals who have a negative impact on your life. These people can be your friends, coworkers, or even family members. If you are interested in developing your self-esteem, you should work hard to surround yourself with those who do bring some positivity to your life. Positive energy will affect you, and you will feel better. Stop thinking that your life is happy or sad. Your life is all about making choices that make you happy or sad.

Do you feel that only a few people have positive self-esteem? If you think so, then you are wrong! Like any other personality trait, self-esteem can be developed. If you feel left behind or if you feel like your self-esteem was hurt, then you can work on improving it.

However, before you can concentrate on improving your self-esteem, you must be aware of the reasons that reduce your self-esteem.

Are you a good judge of yourself? Are you capable of taking negative criticism from those around you and are you capable of accepting your mistakes? Can you work on improving yourself based on the criticism you receive, or do you get defensive or depressed? Do you understand that a portion of the comments you receive from someone isn't representative of the general opinion that others have of you?

Can you accept your uniqueness? You might wish to be taller, slimmer, more outgoing, and less impulsive. However, whenever you ask yourself "who am I?", do you have an answer to it that takes into consideration your uniqueness? Even after a tiring day, can you maintain good body posture, or do you slouch? Would you consider yourself to be optimistic or pessimistic? Do you like wearing clothes that you want or are your choices influenced by what others think of you? Do you do things for your satisfaction or because someone else has asked you to do a particular job?

Take some time out, and answer the questions mentioned above honestly. Everyone would have faced some instance or another in their life that reduced their self-esteem. It is quite natural. However, it is essential to build it back and not let your self-esteem plummet further. Like any other personality trait, even self-esteem can be improved.

How to know if hope actually exists for your struggling marriage or if it is beyond recovery.

Calm your mind

You can call your intuition an intimate knowledge or innate understanding of something. It refers to that tiny voice in your head that is always trying to communicate with you. The problem, though, is that it can be quite difficult to hear it until your mind is calm and the loud mental chatter comes to a halt. Most people tend to have an overactive mind and tend to associate too much with their thoughts. Your thoughts don't control or define you. Instead, you must be able to control your thoughts. You need to remember that you are much more than you think. Once you've learned to reduce or eliminate mental chatter, you can easily access your intuition.

Find a quiet place, close the door, turn the phone off or put it on silent, and physically distance yourself from all devices. Then take a few deep and relaxing breaths. Concentrate on inhaling and exhaling. Whenever thoughts float in your head, imagine them

151

as clouds floating in the sky. Then you can redirect your attention and concentrate on your breathing. Call it meditation if you like, but it's an excellent technique to calm the mind. When your mind is calm, you can think better and listen to your intuition again. Not just that, it also helps you think more rationally.

Listen to your intuition

Pay attention to what your instincts tell you, especially when you meet someone for the first time. Your body is good at understanding the vibes you get from others. It might not be a full-fledged science, but it does help you get a read on things and the people around you. Pay attention to what you feel as soon as you meet someone; focus on the instant reaction you feel before you have even had the time to think. This will help you to understand whether you are comfortable with someone or not.

Pay attention to your body signals

Your body tends to provide you with information about your health, the decisions you make, and others around you. Learn to start paying attention to these signals that your body keeps giving. It means that you must rest when tired, cry when you are sad, eat when you are hungry, and take a break when you are stressed out. It also means that you should start taking note of those around you who help to boost your energy levels and those who extinguish them. You can use this information while deciding whether someone is a good influence on you or not. This will help you limit your contact with people who feel toxic.

You have to choose between "happiness" and staying together, right? Wrong! How to pave the path to happiness inside your marriage if that's what you want.

Dealing with a narcissist is something that truly takes practice. They are different than those without narcissism, and since this is not an issue that you deal with frequently with multiple people, there is a learning curve. The most important thing is to never discount yourself for them. This is what they want, but there are ways to recognize this and ensure that you are creating and maintaining the right boundaries.

Take a step back and analyze the situation.

Determine how bad the situation is. Try to understand the narcissist's background and the degree of his narcissism. Note or recall what drives him to narcissistic rage. Recall how he tries to punish you. Be aware of the tactics that he uses. Do all these objectively. Being carried away by emotions, shouting or crying will only feed the narcissist. The narcissist has already painstakingly set up a strong image or reputation and you might not come across as credible when you tell others, so you have to do your homework.

Accept that the narcissist will not change.

Hoping that you will be able to knock some sense into the narcissist or that you could explain things to enlighten him will not work. As far as the narcissist is concerned, he has done no wrong.

Seek help.

Find people – friends, counselors, religious leaders, or parents - anyone you can confide in and who can give advice and emotional support. They can also give feedback from a neutral viewpoint.

Relaxation

Relaxation is an important part of everyone's lives, including the narcissist. But for those who are dating or married to a narcissist, friends with one, or the narcissist happens to be your mother or father, finding time to get away from the hounding madness that usually ensues when in their company is a valuable asset in managing your emotional and mental strength. Constantly listening can switch you off, make you feel unmotivated, and hurt you. It can drive you mad and can drive you away in tears. But finding somewhere where you can essentially switch off and switch back on again is paramount, like hiking, running, or beach walks. Clarity is the best natural and mental healer. It allows for storage space to be freed up and offers you the platform to think. Reading a book, listening to music, cooking - there are so many forms of relaxation that can really refresh someone. Renew yourself away from the narcissistic atmosphere and remove yourself from the narcissistic environment in which you live or work. Even if this is for ten minutes, finding that balance again is important when dealing with a narcissist.

Be realistic.

Know the narcissist's limitations and work within those limits. It will only be emotionally draining and a waste of time to expect more from the narcissist than he is capable. Do not expect him to learn to care because he can't. Remember that your value as a person does not depend on the narcissist.

Don't punish yourself for getting into a relationship with him. Instead, focus on rebuilding your self-esteem, meeting your own needs and pursuing your interests.

Speak to them in a way that will make them aware of how they will benefit.

Instead of voicing you needs, pleading, crying or yelling; learn to rephrase your statements by emphasizing what the narcissist will gain from it. You have learned to appeal to their selfishness. This is a good way to survive in situations when you cannot leave.

Do Not Give in to Their Fantasy

A narcissist builds a fantasy life, and when dealing with them, it is important to not fall for the fantasy. They can be charming so it can be hard to resist them. It does not take long to essentially get lost in their web. At first, you might feel important, special and important to them, but this never lasts. Keep the following in mind concerning not falling for the fantasy:

They will not fulfill your needs. In fact, what you need and want will not even be recognized, so it is important to keep this in mind. A narcissist views your value as what you can do for them and what you can do to satiate their ego.

Pay close attention to how they treat other people. You will be able to see that they are not afraid to manipulate, lie, disrespect and hurt other people.

Eventually, this behavior and treatment will trickle down to you.

Make sure that you do not forget about your dreams. When you are close to a narcissist, it is easy to get swept up in their delusions and fantasy. It is important that you do not lose yourself in this or else you may find it hard to regain control over who you are.

Set Your Boundaries and Stick to Them

If you have had a relationship with a narcissist for a while, you surely can see their pattern of not respecting your boundaries. To change this, make a plan. This plan should be based on what you hope to achieve by making it. Then, consider how you will enforce the plan and what the consequences will be should the narcissist violate your boundaries. The most important thing about your plan is that you stand firm and that you do not give in to the needs of the narcissist. Make sure to let them know when your boundaries have been crossed.

Be prepared for relationship changes. A narcissist is not a big fan of people not admiring them and giving into their every whim. They want to call all of the shots, and they want you to prop them up. Once you start creating boundaries, how they treat you is likely

157

to change because they will not be happy about you standing up for yourself. They may try to punish you, demean you, or they might go in the opposite direction and use fake charm to try and manipulate you into going back to give them what they want.

You need to set boundaries. If you want the process of healing to begin, you must establish a protective wall around yourself. If you can put physical distance between yourself and the narcissist, that's great! Memories related to the narcissist and the relationship will certainly trigger pain and other unpleasant emotions that in turn will slow down your progress. So, cut off all ties with the narcissist. You can block that individual on social media, your phone, and even an email list. It is time to get rid of all the things that remind you of the narcissist. It is time to remove all traces of connection with the narcissist.

If you cannot physically distance yourself from the narcissists, then you can use a simple technique known as the grey rock. The idea is quite simple: While interacting with narcissists, you must disengage yourself mentally as well as emotionally. Even though you might be boiling with rage within, don't let the narcissists see that they can affect you. Once you are alone and in a safe space, you can let your emotions out. You can cry, shout, scream, and do anything that gives you relief.

Another simple way in which you can start establishing boundaries is by saying no. By learning and practicing saying no, you can work on developing your self-respect as well as self-confidence. Your boundary is like a firewall that keeps all malware out while protecting what's within. You must become selective about all those you let in; after all, your mind is a sacred space.

Avoid Taking Things Personally

This will be one of the hardest things that you do, but it is important. A narcissist is not purposely trying to hurt you. This is just who they are, and they are unable to see the faults in their behavior. Remember that their actions, behaviors, and emotions are not about you. This is all about them.

A narcissist will try and create a version of you that is easiest for them to control. It is important that you work on your self-esteem and know your worth so that their view of you does not become how you see yourself. Let them keep their own negativity and do not allow it to change how you feel about yourself.

Find a Good Support System

A narcissist is never going to be a good support

person for you. However, you do need support when you are dealing with someone like this in your life. If they are close to you and have been in your life for a while, the first step is learning what a healthy relationship is. It is about mutual respect and give and take. With a narcissist, you only give, and they only take.

Focus your time on those that give you love, respect, and honesty. This will help you to see who you truly are so that you do not have to get approval from the narcissist in your life.

Start to break away from the person. A narcissist wants all the attention on them, so they often try to isolate those they want to keep to themselves. This makes it easier for them to gain control over you. Spend time meeting new people or reconnecting with friends you might have lost touch with.

Seek out meaningful opportunities and activities. Consider going for that promotion you have wanted, volunteer or try a new hobby. When you have a fulfilling life, this acts as a natural support system for you.

Make Sure to Stay Positive

Narcissists feed on watching other people feel bad, so

even if they do cause you to experience negative emotions, do not let them see this. When you are around them, make sure that you are in a positive mindset. No matter how hard they try to bring you down, keep a smile on your face and do not react to them.

Know That They Need Help

Narcissism is a mental health issue that someone cannot just will away. They will need help if they ever expect to get their behavior under control. If you approach them and recommend they reach out to a professional, they are unlikely to just agree and go. They may even become angry or defensive due to you even suggesting it. If you care about the person and want them to at least consider help, approach the subject gently and know that this is something that you will likely have to discuss several times before they will even consider it.

Freeing Yourself from Negative Emotions

Anger, jealousy, envy and other negative emotions can permeate your life and cause significant problems. It is important to recognize their existence and then work to be free of them. Freeing yourself from such emotions is a process, and it takes time. Even after you free yourself, you will need to commit to long-term work and maintenance.

Negative emotions are powerful and can quickly become habits if you do not get them under control. For example, if you commonly respond to criticism with anger, over time, this repetition will cause you to become angry any time you are criticized. This can start to impact your relationships, your career and other elements of your life.

Stop Making Excuses

When you make excuses for negative emotions, either for yourself or others, you are telling yourself that they are something out of your control. This is not true because you have the choice concerning how you react to a situation. If you continue to make excuses, you will never take responsibility for your behavior. Over time, this can start to push people out of your life because they will not want to be around someone who cannot admit their faults or when they are wrong.

Take Responsibility

Once you dedicate yourself to no longer making excuses, you can start to take some responsibility for how you act in various situations. This starts by taking the power away from your negative emotions.

As you continue to take responsibility, you will find that they lose their hold over you. The right reactions and choices will naturally start to become easier to make.

Let It Go

Life would be much simpler if everything could be controlled, but this is not possible. When you find something that you have no control over, recognize it and let it go. For example, not every person will like you, and there are times when a loved one may get mad at you for something that is not your fault. Do not press the issue. Let it go, and everything will eventually work itself out in the end.

There are simpler things that you can start doing on a regular basis to start pushing out negative emotions and helping to enhance your overall well-being. You do not have to do every single one on a daily basis but consider them and incorporate them into your day when it is appropriate.

Get your Life Back on Track

It can be tricky to stop dwelling on the past and to stop thinking about all the pain the narcissistic abuse caused. You need to stop pondering the past and instead focus on the bright future ahead.

163

Experiencing pain is the natural response to abuse, and it might have also damaged your sense of self. So, you are dealing with a lot. Getting your life back on track after a narcissistic injury or after ending a relationship with a narcissist is not an easy task. There exists a cognitive discord between two ideas that causes a lot of confusion when the relationship ends. One part of your brain might still be thinking about the narcissist as your soulmate while the other part views him as your ex. This discord causes confusion, and often those who were victims of narcissistic abuse or were in a toxic relationship with a narcissist are usually in disbelief. It's disbelief that someone they trusted violated his trust and abused his love.

Eliminate all toxicity

In the past, you might have done everything you possibly could to please and appease the narcissist you were with. This can take a serious toll on your mental health. You might have subjected yourself to a lot of toxicity by trying to "understand" the narcissist and by trying to walk in his shoes. Narcissists are not only aware of the control they have over their victims, but they also exploit this empathic trait.

Now, it is time to get all this toxicity out of your

system so you can start thinking clearly once again. The best idea is to start externalizing it. You can start maintaining a journal to write about what you have been through, talk to those friends you trust, consult a therapist, or even join a support group. Joining a support group is a good idea because it will help connect you with others who have experienced all that you did. Externalizing the toxicity you were subjected to will help get rid of any confusion you have and help you see things clearly once again. You can start thinking rationally and logically after getting rid of all the dark goo that once resided in your mind. Apart from this, you can also use physical activity as a means of externalizing the toxicity.

Focus

There will certainly be times when you feel like your past is drawing you in. The combination of cognitive discord and the trauma bond you shared with the narcissist are the reason for this. If you feel like this, it means that you are yet to understand and process some emotions. It is quintessential you keep working to overcome the abuse you were a victim of. Instead of letting your past rob you of your present, allocate some time for yourself where you can analyze your past.

Until then, you need to keep practicing mindfulness.

165

Whatever has happened must stay in the past. It must not ruin your present or your future. Stay in the present and concentrate on creating an amazing future for yourself. Ensure that you have a sense of purpose in life and are looking forward to bringing about a positive change in your life. Instead of dwelling on the past, it is time to move forward and keep going without looking back.

Be patient

You must be patient with yourself. You cannot hurry up and rush through the process of recovery. There will be times when you feel like you are staring at a bottomless pit of despair; you might get frustrated or might even feel quite depressed. Well, this merely means you need to concentrate on healing yourself.

The very first thing you should do if and when you realize the marriage is over.

You will also undergo a period of distress, akin to mourning when you leave. Seek help and support to get through this stage. Do not be hard on yourself for having allowed yourself to be deceived by the narcissist. Your experience will make you stronger, wiser and, in time, ready for a healthy relationship. In the meantime, focus on your own interests and rebuilding your self-esteem.

Isn't this a statement you tell yourself every day!? It plays in your mind like a mantra, the self-affirmation reminding you that going in the right direction will be worth it in the end. It should be so easy - why stay with someone who has no empathy, care or kindness towards you and who wants to see you suffer? Yet it is not a easy as it seems, hence why you need to repeat statements such as this.

Divorce is a serious thing. The process inevitably means that you have decided to part ways, restart your life and take back your individual resources, belongings and physical necessities. This in itself is a major red flag in a codependent-narcissist relationship! Your partner's entire identity is merged in the reality that he or she can feed off you, use you as their hidden and subtle yet powerful support system, and bounce off your kindness, empathy and positive attributes. So, once you starting responding this destroys their world. They can no longer keep up the facade once you make the decision that their actions are not acceptable. This can **only** happen when you begin to respond.

True response begins when you start to slow down and become an observer of both your own thoughts and feelings and your partner's. This is best achieved through **meditation** and **mindfulness**. The significance of these two self-help methods cannot be overlooked. They are both extremely powerful in helping you to live your best life, be free from narcissistic abuse or targeting, and to start responding.

The hardest battle you will fight is not one for your recovery. It's the fight for your right to leave the narcissist. Creating physical, mental and emotional distance between you and the narcissist are crucial aspects of the recovery process. They will never make it easy, and getting away from them may be a very traumatizing experience - especially when you don't know what you're dealing with. Unfortunately, there is no easy way out and we have to face the narcissist in their injured and enraged state if we wish to be free.

In essence, mindfulness can help you see the light and recognize that your mind is a powerful tool. You are not responsible for your partner's thoughts, behaviors, actions or inactions, but you do have control over your own.

This is one thing that many people don't tell you when taking the steps to divorce a narcissist. You need mantras or affirmation-like statements to keep you on course, remind you that this really is in your best interest, and that it will be worth it in the end.

The psychological, mental and emotional abuse and trauma you have suffered are real, and regardless of how many times you have been gas-lighted, or made to appear crazy, in the wrong or losing the plot, you know the truth in the core of your cells. Being with a narcissist is completely detrimental to your health.

If you feel yourself becoming stressed, anxious, nervous or heated inside, these are sure signs that you are on the verge of a reaction. Unlike in partnerships where narcissism is not present or a key theme, and where most people are allowed a few moments of blowing off steam or showing weakness; in this relationship you are not provided the patience, compassion or support necessary. This means that even when or if your partner does happen to be in a serene, kind or non-narcissistic space you may unfortunately spark them with your own reactive behaviors. It is extremely rare for a true narcissist to see you becoming upset or worked up on your own accord and not use it as a chance for drama, or further manipulation.

You get the idea. The moment you leave the narcissist, but have to keep in touch with them for whatever reason, your life will be under inspection. The narcissist will be quick to assume details about your private life and paint a dirty picture. If you fall for this trick, they'll have you hooked and you'll continue to be their narcissistic supply. Your attempts to correct their wrong assumptions will make them feel superior and will only lead to more negative comments.

Narcissistic abuse hasn't just made us feel bad about ourselves. It's actually changed the way we think. Yes, those negative and hurtful thoughts will sit with you and pop up into your mind when you're feeling down. Aside from the internalized voice of the narcissist constantly putting us down, narcissistic abuse has changed how we view others and how we process what they have to say. It's easy to end up being affected by our abusers without even realizing that it was them who introduced and reinforced certain thought processes in our minds.

Managing conflict is the same if not similar to learning how to respond. When dealing with someone with deeply buried narcissism, you need to know how to respond appropriately and in a way that doesn't cause further harm to yourself. Once again, you are not responsible for the narcissist's energy. You may have spent years being the most patient, loyal, loving and understanding or empathetic partner, yet these qualities are all lost on them. Managing conflict during or after the divorce proceedings should not be viewed as any different.

Please do not make the mistake of thinking that now you are finally free, or soon to be free, that your partner will suddenly 'see sense' or have a heartfelt awakening. They will not. A narcissist will always view you as their scapegoat and wall or mirror to project their stuff onto, so now you are taking the correct steps and working towards your own wellbeing and happiness; they do not want to let go or give you up so easy.

The following steps may seem simple or effortlessly implemented, yet they are not! Narcissists will do everything in their power to maintain their illusion of power, and try to keep you entrapped in their games until it really is all over. So, in order to combat this and manage conflict successfully, do stay committed and completely aligned to the following. They are all necessary for your happiness, peace of mind and success.

Kindness, Tolerance & Self-Respect

Above anything else you need to have self-respect. This links with kindness and tolerance, which are both necessary to manage and deal with conflict harmoniously. The self-respect part is the trinity due to the fact that you won't receive much kindness or respect from your partner, unfortunately. However, you should seek to remain kind and tolerant during the process. There is great truth in the validity of the power or law of attraction. We attract, magnetize and harmonize to us what we give out, so any energy or intentions we project we will receive. If you are sending out harmful, hurtful or separation based vibrations - you shall receive more from your partner. In other words, you cannot fight chaos and narcissism with more destruction or ill wishes! Showing kindness and respect, even if in neutral and indifferent civil ways, will allow you to remain sane, clear headed and calm; also enabling you to stay as clear as possible from your partner's detrimental motivations.

Being Your Own Best Friend, Lover and Soulmate

To succeed, you need to be your own best friend, lover and soulmate. You need to practice self-love and show up for yourself (because your narcissistic partner isn't going to). Managing conflict is not just about what you can do for the other person or situation as a whole, but it is about what you can do for yourself. Being your best self for you allows you to be your best self for others. Even if your partner is incapable of rationality or niceness, this commitment to being the best version of you still has a positive effect. Subtle energy and intentions are real, and showing up for yourself in a way which states that you are self-loving, self-respecting and not going to tolerate anything less than harmonious and ethical cooperation, means that the situation will flow better than if you didn't commit to these things. Your vibe projects outwards, also influencing physical reality and the experiences you attract. How divorce or separation proceedings go can all be changed and shaped by your mindset.

Conclusion

T hank you for making it through to the end of this book. You might have dealt with one in the past or are dealing with one now. If you don't want the narcissist to control your life and dictate every action of yours, then you need to learn to deal with him. There are various steps you can take to sever all ties with a narcissist and regain control of your life. It is time you take action, put your foot down and get your life back on track.

With the help of the information provided in this book, you will be able to identify a narcissist quickly. Once you can identify him, it becomes easier to deal with him and take corrective action. You can prevent yourself from becoming a narcissist's pawn. Now, all that you must do is take action immediately and deal with the narcissist in your life.

If cutting contact from a narcissist is not possible, other techniques may be employed to make life easier, and avoid infuriating or upsetting them. Avoiding being in their inner circle, whilst remaining warm and approving allows a safe distance to be maintained - making attack or upset far less likely.

Causing unnecessary injury to their ego through exposing them as abusive or less than they think themselves to be, rejecting them or outshining them is likely to backfire and cause a great deal of commotion. If peace is the main objective, understanding and avoiding these triggers is preferable.

Get all the support you can get either through a private therapist or a support group. Be easy on yourself as well and stand strong to your emotions and your needs. As you move forward take what you have learned from this book and do what is best for you in your life.

Lastly, as you navigate this painful process, do not feel discouraged if you slip up. You are not perfect, and that is okay! Recognizing that fact is one of the key features that separates you from a narcissist. It is okay to recognize and acknowledge our weaknesses and faults. Understanding them only makes us more capable as people. Only the narcissist will expect perfection, and that is due to his own distorted thinking. Do not expect perfection from yourself. It is okay to fail sometimes. When you mess up or slip up, the best thing you can do is pick yourself up, remind yourself that you are doing okay, and keep moving forward. You are more than capable of healing from the narcissist's abuse with a little perseverance and guidance.

CPSIA information can be obtained
at www.ICGtesting.com
Printed in the USA
BVHW061552261020
591850BV00012B/1125